BLUE GUIDE

HAY-ON-WYE

Robin Saikia

Somerset Books • London

First edition 2010

Published by Blue Guides Limited, a Somerset Books Company
Winchester House, Deane Gate Avenue, Taunton, Somerset TA1 2UH
www.blueguides.com
'Blue Guide' is a registered trademark

ISBN 978–1–905131–37–2

A CIP catalogue record of this book is available from the British Library

Distributed in the United States of America by
WW Norton and Company, Inc.
500 Fifth Avenue, New York, NY 10110

The author and editor have made reasonable efforts to ensure the accuracy
of all the information in *Blue Guide Hay-on-Wye*; however, they can accept
no responsibility for any loss, injury or inconvenience sustained by any
traveller as a result of information or advice contained in the guide.

Statement of editorial independence: Blue Guides, their authors and
editors, are prohibited from accepting any payment from any restaurant,
hotel, gallery or other establishment for its inclusion in this guide or on
www.blueguides.com, or for a more favourable mention than would
otherwise have been made.

All other acknowledgements, photo credits and copyright information
are given on p. 160, which forms part of this copyright page.

CONTENTS

INTRODUCTION

Hay-on-Wye is a market town in the Upper Wye Valley, on the border of England and Wales, internationally famous for its unusual but thriving micro-economy of book-dealers, hoteliers, restaurateurs, farmers, artists and literati. Variously described as 'Paradise' (John Masefield), 'Purgatory' (Howard Jacobson) and 'Hell' (Joe Stretch), it combines the more winning aspects of all three in abundant and appealing measure. One of the high points in the Hay year is the Guardian Hay Festival (full title The Guardian Hay Festival of Literature and the Arts), which takes place for ten days at the end of May and the beginning of June, described by Bill Clinton as a 'Woodstock of the mind'. This and the year-long endeavours of the thriving second-hand book industry keep the town in the international news and stimulate its other businesses, its pubs, restaurants and shops. There is also a quiet but well-established rural economy, driven by farmers, craftsmen and other ancillary tradesmen, which functions independently of the glitz, glamour and hurly-burly of the arts.

Hay characters

Throughout a colourful history dating back to the Norman conquest, Hay-on-Wye has seen a fair number of major and minor historical figures come and go. These include William de Braose (the 'Ogre of Abergavenny'), the Welsh nationalist leader Owain Glyndwr, the Lollard rebel Sir John Oldcastle, George Psalmanazar 'The Great Formosan

View of Hay Clock Tower, looking north.

View of Castle Street from the top of the Castle steps.

Impostor', the American writer W.D. Howells, Bruce Chatwin the novelist, and April Ashley, Britain's first transsexual. The best-known Hay character of recent years is Richard Booth, owner of Hay Castle, who from modest beginnings in 1961–62 built up a massive book business in the town. Booth crowned himself King of Hay on April Fools' Day 1977. This protest against what he saw as the parsimony and corruption of local and central government was also a shrewd publicity move which soon elevated him to cult status and put Hay on the international stage. The new king bestowed peerages and printed passports; but underlying the media farrago and flim-flam lay Booth's passionate conviction that he could regenerate the ailing fortunes of the small market town single-handed. By default a member of the 'Establishment'—educated miserably, he claims, at Rugby and Merton College, Oxford—Booth una-

shamedly 'ruled' his kingdom along feudal lines. He is now in semi-retirement, devoting his energies to promoting the concept of the 'Booktown' worldwide. But he remains an Arthurian presence, ever ready to return to the heartland of Hay should it need him—even though (a recent development) he was decapitated in effigy by a breakaway group of what he called 'revolting' peasants led by book-dealer Peter Harries. The ascent of Hay-on-Wye as a 'Booktown' brought about the Hay Festival, founded by the Florence acting dynasty on the proceeds of a poker game (*see p. 85*). Other players who have invested in Hay include the developer Leon Morelli and the philanthropist Hilary Lawson.

Origins of the name

The town was not known as Hay-on-Wye until 1947. Residents say 'Hay' and newcomers soon follow their lead, abandoning the awkwardness of the hyphenated civic neologism. Purists say 'The Hay', harking back to Geoffrey Fairs's definitive book, *A History of the Hay*. Hay, it should be noted, does not derive from the word for dried grass but rather from the Norman French *haie*, meaning a walled or fenced enclosure. Although it bears an English postcode, Hay has a distinctly Anglo-Welsh identity and a Welsh name, Y Gelli, meaning 'The Grove'—sticklers will refer to Y Gelli Gandryll, the 'Grove of a Hundred Plots'. Despite the long and complex history of confrontation between Welsh and English on the borders, the community in Hay is noticeably relaxed about the rivalry. If anything, English and Welsh residents will tend to unite against perceived threats from the outside world—predatory property developers, absentee landlords, Johnny-come-lately celebrities and the like—rather than turn on one another. The town wears its commercial success well. Even grumblers amongst the book dealers grumble from a position of prosperity—born of low overheads—that is the envy of their counterparts elsewhere in Britain, particularly in London.

Layout of the town

Hay forms a triangle, bounded on the south by Oxford Road, on the west by Belmont Road and Broad Street and to the east by Heol y Dwr and Lion Street. Within this triangle there is a pleasing criss-cross of winding streets and lanes dominated by the Castle and its outbuildings. There are several sites of architectural and historical interest, the principals being Hay Castle, Memorial Square, the Butter Market, the Cheese Market, the Town Clock, the Three Tuns pub and the Guild Chapel of St John the Baptist. The overall feel is of a market town that developed gradually

Plaque on Castle Street, on the site of one of the three medieval town gates.

over the centuries, one school of architecture making ramshackle way for the next. Early timber-framed buildings sit amicably side by side with appealing examples of early 19th-century Classicism and the occasional Victorian Gothic status symbol such as the Clock Tower.

Falling outside the triangle to the west are the Parish Church of St Mary, the nearby Norman motte, The Swan Inn, Hay-on-Wye Cemetery and the Hay Union Workhouse. The many bookshops, most with a few exceptions located within the triangle, are easy to find and well signposted, as are a thriving mix of galleries, craft shops, boutiques, pubs and restaurants.

Hay's stretch of the Wye Valley Walk can be picked up at St Mary's Church, following the Wye northeast as far as Wyeford Road then backtracking southeast to rejoin the town at the Old Black Lion Inn. The Offa's Dyke Path runs south over the fields from Oxford Road, beneath the Castle walls, and northeast along the north bank of the Wye.

The Tourist Information Centre is located in the Craft Centre by the car park to the south of Oxford Road.

HISTORICAL SKETCH

Though the first signs of human habitation in the Hay area come some 5,000 years ago in the Bronze and Iron Ages, the first settlers tended to avoid low-lying areas and kept to the high ground. The river bank at The Warren would have been a wild place, a thicket of tangled undergrowth, home to beavers, bears, wild cats and boars. There is little evidence of Roman settlement, though Francis Kilvert owned an Augustan denarius that had been found 'near Hay'. There are the remains of a fort near Clyro, on a well-defended site immediately east of Clyro Castle (*see p. 110*), but this is north of the Wye and outside the boundaries of Hay. The Romans had as their foe the formidable Silures tribe, described by their historian Raymond Howell as 'a resilient and sophisticated clan-based tribal confederation' and by Tacitus as *non atrocitate, non clementia mutabatur* (unmoveable either by force or mercy). These dark-haired tribesmen—they share DNA with the Basques and other peoples of northern Spain and southern France—are the ancestors of the modern Welsh. Their descendants were the intractable people the Normans had to contend with when they set about colonising the Welsh Marches.

The struggle to control the border

Hay owes its existence to the Norman Conquest and the complex struggle for power and preferment that prevailed in the Welsh border country from c. 1100 onwards.

View of Offa's Dyke, the 8th-century ditch and rampart that guarded the border of England and Wales.

OFFA OF MERCIA & 'OFFA'S DYKE'

The Christian king Offa of Mercia (757–96) was one of the most powerful early rulers in Britain. His frequent conflicts with the Welsh were the inspiration for the 'Dyke', an earth-built border fortification spectacular in terms of the manpower and organisation that would have been required to build it. The design is simple: a high ridge on the Mercian side afforded Offa's men a vantage point, while a deep ditch on the Powys side formed an impediment to the Welsh aggressor. There is some controversy over exactly how defensible such a fortification would have been against a concerted invasion, but there is no doubt as to the Dyke's effectiveness as a tangible symbol of the Welsh-English divide. We learn from Asser's *Life of Alfred* that 'a certain vigorous

A slight rise in the land indicates the former presence of a Roman fort, on Boatside Farm above the Offa's Dyke Path.

king called Offa had a great dyke built between Wales and Mercia from sea to sea'. We learn from George Borrow's *Wild Wales* that it 'was customary for the English to cut off the ears of every Welshman who was found to the east of the dyke, and for the Welsh to hang every Englishman whom they found to the west of it', a colourful allusion to the anti-Welsh decrees made in the reigns of Egbert and Harold and the resulting reprisals by the Welsh. In the *Gododdin* of Aneirin we meet the warrior Issac, who is 'well-mannered over mead' but whose sword 'rings yet in the ears of mothers' when he 'strides the Rampart of Offer'. Nowadays it is the name of Simon Rayner that rings yet in the ears of mothers. He is Membership Secretary of the Offa's Dyke Association, an independent group that provides information to walkers planning to explore all or part of the 177-mile stretch of Offa's Dyke running from Prestatyn to Chepstow. The path approximately follows the Wales-England border, passing towns and hamlets, forts, castles and abbeys and taking in spectacular stretches of landscape including the summit of the Black Mountains. The route passes through Hay and is marked on the map on p. 158.

Offa's Dyke enthusiasts can be fractious in their views, some holding that only parts of the earthwork can be attributed to Offa. They are nevertheless united in thinking that the dyke is a British achievement and it is therefore inadvisable in their company to advance the idea (over mead?) that it was in reality built by the Roman Emperor Septimius Severus in about AD 200. This notion, based on passages in Eutropius' *Historiae Romanum Breviarum* of 369, used to have some currency but is now discredited.

The Romans had been fully aware of the turbulence on the borders and had been content simply to exploit the iron and coal resources of the Wye Valley, abandoning any idea of further territorial expansion after difficult confrontations with the formidable Silures. Offa, similarly, had done little more than build his Dyke from north to south, demarcating the border between Wales and England.

The Normans, by contrast, were aggressive, keen to subdue and fortify the region, and they hit on a crude but effective way of tackling the problem, selecting groups of ambitious warlords and inviting them to carve out territories for themselves on the Welsh borders. The appointment of these so-called Marcher Lords had three distinct advantages. Firstly, the king was obliged to do no more than give his blessing to any proposed land-grab; it would not take a toll on his purse. Secondly, a mission in Wales was a convenient way of getting rid of potentially threatening subjects, aggressive personalities who might prove a challenge to authority if harboured closer to home. Thirdly, upon the successful conquest of the border territory, strategic alliances could be made, mostly through marriage, that would strengthen the position of the monarch in the borders, in time intermingling Welsh with Norman-Angevin blood. A crucial moment in Anglo-Welsh history—and a key to the understanding of Hay and places like it—is recorded in the *Brut y Tywysogion* (*The Chronicle of the Princes*) and is worth quoting in full for the light it sheds on Norman strategy in the Marches: 'And the king [Henry I] said to Gilbert [FitzRichard of Clare]: "You were always pestering me for a portion of Wales. Now I will give to you the land of Cadwgan ap Bleddyn [King of Powys in mid-Wales]. Go and take possession of it". And he gladly accepted it from the king. And then, gathering a host, along with his comrades he came to Ceredigion [Cardigan]. And he took possession of it, and built two castles there.'

This, then, was the accepted form: the warlord, with the king's patronage, would assemble a private army and set out for Wales, to carve out for himself a prestigious and profitable fiefdom.

Hay under the Normans

Hay owes its existence to the Norman warlord Bernard of Neufmarché, a resourceful adventurer who in the 1080s began successful forays into the Wye Valley. Though he joined a rebellion against William Rufus, he and other rebels were granted amnesty on condition that they made some tangible recompense to their king. Bernard vigorously entered into the pact, defeating the Welsh king Bleddyn at the Battle of Brecon in 1093. Hay was established as a key border fortification and placed in the charge of William Revel, one of Bernard's retainers. The parish church of St Mary was dedicated in 1115, and it is from that point onwards that the town steadily grew, as English and Anglo-Norman tenants were enticed to settle in the turbulent border area by the grant of reasonable leases on burgages, generous plots of land. Though the fortunes of its overlords for the next 400 years were never less than dramatic, Hay quietly developed a level of prosperity and self-sufficiency as a market town that has persisted, with temporary doldrums, to the present day.

The reign of the Neufmarchés, however, was short-lived. Bernard's son Mahael was disinherited after an unpleasant intrigue that tells us much about the imaginative and expedient dispensation of justice prevalent at the time. According

to the chronicler Gerald of Wales, Mahael discovered that
his mother, Nesta, had been enjoying a secret affair. He set
about giving her lover a ferocious beating, no doubt assum-
ing this to be a straightforward way of restoring family
honour. Nesta, however, was a formidable woman who did
not take her son's intervention lightly. Her aristocratic lineage was impeccable: her father was a Norman, Osbern
Fitzrichard, Sheriff of Hereford, and on her mother's side
she was descended from the Welsh prince Gruffydd ap
Llywelyn. As such, she was a typical product of the classic
Norman-Welsh marriage alliance and someone whose feel-
ings were likely to be taken seriously. When she com-
plained of her son's behaviour to Henry I, she sealed
Mahael's fate by making the unsettling disclosure that he
was not the son of Bernard after all but of another of her
lovers. The king stripped Mahael of Hay and his other
estates in Brecon, conferring them on Mahael's sister, Sibyl.
The king then married Sibyl to his friend and supporter
Miles of Gloucester, High Constable of England, thus
ensuring that Hay, along with other strategically important
land, passed by marriage into safe and loyal hands.

Miles was an energetic warlord but his tenure of Hay did
not last long. Though he supported Matilda in her war
against King Stephen and afterwards survived Matilda's
defeat, rising to become Earl of Hereford, his trajectory was
cut short when he was accidentally shot in the Forest of
Dean by one of his hunting companions. Miles had been an
ambitious and enterprising man, described drily by the
worldly-wise commentator John of Salisbury as *non tam
comites regni quam hostes publici*: not so much a friend of the
king as an enemy of the people. After his death, Miles was
succeeded by four of his sons in turn, in whose hands Hay

passed through comparatively uneventful times. They all died leaving no heirs and eventually the Brecon-Hay portion of the estate was inherited by their sister Bertha, whose husband was William de Braose of Builth.

The de Braose overlordship

There follows a colourful period in Hay history, the high points of which are to be found in the tenure of William de Braose (or Breos), son of William and Bertha. William's enduring claim to fame is the so-called Abergavenny Massacre of 1175. Suspecting that his uncle, Henry Fitzmiles, had been murdered by the Welsh leader Seisyll ap Dyfnwal, he invited Seisyll and other leading Welsh figures to a Christmas feast at Abergavenny, Christmas being a traditional time of reconciliation among the Welsh. Once the guests were safely at ease, William murdered them. If Miles of Gloucester had been a subtle intriguer, William and his wife, Maud de St Valery (nicknamed Maud Walbee), were border warlords in the old tradition. William vigorously set about expanding his empire in southeast Wales, an expansion that was marked by the defeat of the Welsh at Painscastle in 1198 when English troops under the joint command of de Braose and Geoffrey Fitzpeter mustered at Hay Castle prior to the battle. Maud (also known as Matilda), who rallied the troops at Painscastle, was also a force to be reckoned with. In local lore she attained something of a magical status that harks back in flavour to the pre-Christian myths of the *Mabinogion*. The myth that she was a giantess who built Hay Castle in one night is an enduring one: she is said to have pitched a loose stone caught in her shoe, in fact a gigantic menhir, over the Wye where it now rests in Llowes churchyard (*map p. 156, B1*).

In 1199 John was crowned king and the de Braoses became firm royal favourites. Rewarded by John with estates and high office in southeast Wales, in addition to those they had already inherited or appropriated, William and Maud seemed assured a bright future until circumstances took an unexpected turn for the worse in 1207.

King John began to question the integrity of his favourites and to claw back a significant portion of the estates with which he had rewarded them. In the case of the de Braoses, the suggestion was that they were withholding or even stealing revenue

Worn effigy in St Mary's church said by popular lore to be 'Maud Walbee', wife of William de Braose, though the figure depicted is in fact male.

from the Crown. At first sight this seemed like a copybook attempt by an anxious monarch, well within his rights, to check the progress of two over-ambitious subjects, but it soon became clear that there was a darker issue. It was rumoured—merely rumoured—that in 1203 William de Braose had seen John murder his nephew Prince Arthur of Brittany, who had been regarded by many as the true heir to the English throne. Given John's reputation for ruthlessness, an assassination would certainly have been plausible. Nothing was ever proven, but in the annals of Margam Abbey it is recorded that John tied a heavy stone to Arthur's body and personally threw him into the River Seine. Others said Arthur had died of shock when a gang of John's men came by night with the intention of castrating him. At all events, Arthur, after a period of imprisonment at Rouen, disappeared and was never seen again. His end might have remained safely in the realm of conjecture had it not been for a dramatic indiscretion. John, increasing his pressure on the de Braoses, demanded that William and Maud send him their sons as hostages as proof of their allegiance. Maud, infuriated by this, publicly accused John of murdering Arthur. The repercussions were swift and terrible. John seized Hay; William, after an unsuccessful attempt at local insurrection orchestrated from Castell Dinas, fled to Ireland; Maud and her eldest son William were captured by John and starved to death by him. William died in exile in France.

A CONTEMPORARY PORTRAIT OF WILLIAM DE BRAOSE

Gerald of Wales, or Giraldus Cambrensis (1146–1223), was born in Pembrokeshire of mixed aristocratic Welsh and Norman ancestry. His uncle was Bishop of St David's and he received a religious education and was appointed chaplain to Henry II in 1184. In 1188 he accompanied the Archbishop of Canterbury, Baldwin of Exeter, on a tour of Wales recruiting for the Third Crusade, which led to him writing the *Itinerarium Cambriae* (1191) and the *Descriptio Cambriae* (1194).

In the *Itinerarium Cambriae* he describes how the Archbishop preached the Crusade at Hay and how many took the Cross. His sardonic remarks on the piety of the much-demonised William de Braose are of considerable ➤

interest. William had 'gravely offended' by keeping to himself revenues that had been granted to the Church—but, according to Gerald, perhaps all was not lost: 'Yet something is to be said in favour of the aforesaid William de Braose, although he greatly offended in this particular (since nothing human is perfect, and to have knowledge of all things, and in no point to err, is an attribute of God, not of man); for he always placed the name of the Lord before his sentences, saying, "Let this be done in the name of the Lord; let that be done by God's will; if it shall please God, or if God grant leave; it shall be so by the grace of God". We learn from Saint Paul, that everything ought thus to be committed and referred to the will of God. On taking leave of his brethren, he says, "I will return to you again, if God permit"; and Saint James uses this expression, "If the Lord will, and we live", in order to show that all things ought to be submitted to the divine disposal. The letters also which William de Braose, as a rich and powerful man, was accustomed to send to different parts, were loaded, or rather honoured, with words expressive of the divine indulgence to a degree not only tiresome to his scribe, but even to his auditors; for as a reward to each of his scribes for concluding his letters with the words, "by divine assistance", he gave annually a piece of gold, in addition to their stipend. When on a journey he saw a church or a cross, although in the midst of conversation either with his inferiors or superiors, from an excess of devotion, he immediately began to pray, and when he had finished his prayers, resumed his conversation. On meeting boys in the way, he invited them by a previous salutation to salute him, that the blessings of these innocents, thus extorted, might be returned to him. His wife, Matilda de Saint Valery, observed all these things: a prudent and chaste woman; a woman placed with propriety at the head of her house, equally attentive to the economical disposal of her property within doors, as to the augmentation of it without; both of whom, I hope, by their devotion obtained temporal happiness and grace, as well as the glory of eternity.'

After William and Maud's fall, there followed a fierce and complicated war of attrition between King John and the remaining de Braoses, who were Giles, Bishop of Hereford and his warrior brother Reginald. The priest and the soldier regained a large portion of family land, a feat they might never have managed without enlisting the support of Llywelyn the Great and the Welsh rulers of Elfael, north of Hay. They had the momentum of the Welsh Uprising of 1211 behind them and were also helped by John's mounting troubles with the barons—but not for long. Eventually John lost patience and set fire to both castle and town in 1215. Given John's record, there might have been more severe reprisals throughout southeast Wales over the years, but the king was soon distracted by problems elsewhere. After his death and the accession of the nine-year-old Henry III under the regency of William Marshall, Earl of Pembroke, Reginald de Braose made peace with his new king, though the era of the de Braoses was marked, fittingly enough, by one further drama. The final William de Braose was hanged by Llywelyn the Great after being found in the bedchamber of Llywelyn's wife, Joan, Princess of

Wales and Lady of Snowdon. The execution, which took place at Aber Garth Celyn (Abergwyngregyn, north Wales) on 2nd May 1230, was remembered with relish by succeeding generations in the local community. William's widow Eva remained in charge at Hay and under her supervision there was a period of settlement and reconstruction (the town walls date to this period) until 1244, when William's estate was divided between the various de Braose heiresses, Eva's daughters.

The de Bohuns

Hay fell to Eleanor, and therefore into the hands of her husband, Humphrey de Bohun, a true Anglo-Norman. Radnor fell to her sister Maud and into the hands of *her* husband, Roger Mortimer, whose lineage formed a potent borders mix, his Ferrers grandmother making up the Norman side and his mother, Princess Gladys, daughter of Llywelyn the Great, the Welsh. There followed a certain amount of inconclusive litigation in which Roger attempted to reduce what he saw as the disproportionate distribution of the estate in favour of the de Bohuns and claim back land, including Hay, for himself. But Roger's hour of reckoning finally came following a new distraction from the ongoing struggle between the Marcher Lords and the Welsh under Llywelyn ap Gruffydd. This was the escalating quarrel between king and barons, in which Mortimer fought with Prince Edward on the king's side against Simon de Montfort who was supported by, amongst many other Norman families, the de Bohuns. Hay passed to and fro between Mortimer and de Bohun until finally, at the Battle of Evesham in 1265, Simon de Montfort was slain, some say by Roger himself. In all events, Simon's body was

Lord High Constable Humphrey de Bohun, together with the Lord Marshal of England, protest to King Edward I about his military demands and high taxation.

carved into pieces which were distributed amongst the victors, Roger receiving the head, which he sent home to Maud at Wigmore Castle. As an additional bonus, Hay reverted to Mortimer, a result far more satisfactory than any he could have obtained in court but which proved to be short-lived, like many an ascendancy in the Marches. The dispossessed barons found a ready champion in the powerful Gilbert de Clare, who had been given by Edward I the seemingly impossible task of reintroducing some stability to the borders. Mortimer was paid appropriate compensation and Hay restored to de Bohun ownership. 1278 saw the final defeat of Llywelyn by Edward I and thereafter, apart from flurries of insurrection, Hay was spared the inconvenience of conflict on its doorstep. The de Bohuns went from strength to strength, obtaining the earldoms of Hereford, Essex and Northampton. One daughter, Mary, was to become the first wife of Henry IV. Her son, Henry V, fought at Agincourt alongside bowmen from Hay. The blood spilt by England in France was a potent mix of the Saxon, Norman and Welsh strains. Mary's elder sister Eleanor, who inherited the lordship of Hay, married Thomas de Woodstock, the youngest son of Edward III. Thanks to well-organised fortification the rebellion of Owain Glyndwr, one of the principal bugbears of Henry IV's reign, touched Hay only peripherally. Although the castle was put on alert in 1402 and supplies were sent in anticipation of a siege, the damage sustained by Hay was minimal compared to the troubles experienced elsewhere in the Marches.

The end of the Middle Ages

From the 15th century, Hay passed to the ill-starred Dukes of Buckingham, the first of whom was Eleanor's grandson Humphrey, created 1st Duke of Buckingham by Henry VI. After careful deliberation he supported the Lancastrian side in the Wars of the Roses and was killed at the Battle of Northampton in 1460. The 2nd Duke of Buckingham was initially a staunch supporter of Richard III and a prime suspect in the murder of the Princes in the Tower. He secretly switched his allegiance to Henry Tudor and after an abortive attempt at a coup, from which he tried to escape in disguise, was beheaded for treason in 1483 in the market square in Salisbury—'there never was falser traitor purveyed for', said Richard. The third duke was executed for treason by Henry VIII in 1521. At Henry's court there was a palpable division between old money and the new men under Wolsey's rising star. Buckingham was widely rumoured to be plotting an aristocratic coup, and a chance remark, to the effect that he was descended from Edward III and that he might well be tempted to add the crown to his many trophies, marked the beginning of the end.

After the third duke's execution, Henry VIII granted the lordship of Hay to James Boyle. From this period onward the town began to enjoy its quiet prosperity. The Union of England and Wales had drastically reduced the military importance of Hay, freeing its citizens to exploit its strategic position as a trading post on the borders. The old divisions between the Englishry of Hay (*Hay Anglicanae*) and its Welshry (*Hay Wallensis*) still existed but rivalries were increasingly forgotten, possibly on account of the excesses of the new regime. On one occasion, James Boyle caused his bailiff to beat up several market stallholders, presumably for holding back on the rent or for 'forestalling', selling goods outside market hours and thus depriving Boyle of his cut. A pedlar, Ewan ap David, recorded in his will his treatment at the hands of Boyle's men: 'I am note sicke by God's visitacioun but by the vilany and hurts received at the handes of William Smythe now baylyf of the Hai.'

At the beginning of the 17th century one of the Boyle girls married Howell Gwynn IV of Trecastle, and the lordship of Hay remained in the Gwynn family for a century. Elizabeth Gwynn, who died in 1702, redeemed the family name by building the Gwynn Almshouses, but it is fair to say that in the early days the Gwynns practised a tyranny that fully chimed with that of the Boyles. Their principal

Industry came to Hay in the early 19th century. Thomas Howells's spinning mill on Bemont Road was one of the town's largest employers.

racket appears to have been the extortion of illegal tolls from visitors to fairs and markets and the illegal imprisonment of those who could not or would not pay.

Commercial growth

In the mid-18th century these tyrannies came to an end on the accession of a new dynasty, the Wellington family. The division of key property in Hay has, at this time, a fluidity more in keeping with the modern age: the Wellingtons bought the Castle, while the actual lordship of Hay had passed into the hands of the Harley family, Earls of Oxford, from which Oxford Street in Hay and the Harley Almshouses take their name. As the 18th century drew to a close, there was a great diversity of commercial and religious activity in Hay that is reflected in its buildings and that reveals itself as one explores the town and considers each of the major landmarks in turn. On the commercial front there was an encyclopaedic diversity of trade: saddlers, peruke-makers, carriers, braziers, watchmakers, builders, tallow chandlers, grocers and more. Thomas Howells's mill (*see box below*) was a leading employer, closely followed by a tannery and later the gasworks and the tramway. On the religious front, with the slow (but only temporary) decline of the Anglican Church in Wales, a multiplicity of Nonconformists came and went or settled, notably Baptists, Calvinistic Methodists, Wesleyan Methodists, Primitive Methodists and Quakers.

Thomas Howells (1749–1819)

Thomas Howells was a prosperous wool and flannel manufacturer who owned three woollen mills in Hay, the largest occupying a site between Castle Street and Belmont Road. It is well known that Thomas visited America in 1808 with his grandson William, the first of the Howells settlers, who went on to become American Consul in Quebec. Thomas's great-grandson, William Dean Howells, was a popular American journalist and travel writer and perhaps the most distinguished of the Howellses who settled in America in the early 19th century.

The purpose of the 1808 visit was to investigate the possibility of setting up a wool manufacturing business. Thomas took with him woollen goods from Hay and letters of introduction to the Governor of Pennsylvania. He was offered ➤

6,000 acres of land near the Potomac River at sixpence an acre but declined, we learn from family records, because his wife Susanna, a genteel woman whom he had met and married in London, did not wish to exchange the comfortable life of Hay for the uncertainties of the Potomac wilderness. Thomas sold his woollen samples and returned to Hay, as local lore has it, with a barrel of silver coins.

What is less widely known is that Thomas had visited America in the past and had contemplated a move there as early as 1789, not long after the Declaration of Independence. In a personal letter to George Washington dated 14th July 1789, Thomas sets out his stall, proposing to start a wool manufacturing business in Virginia (*The Papers of George Washington: Presidential Series 3, pp. 192–96*): 'Last year I visited the Continent of America, with a full determination to become a Settler, but finding the Government not in so settled a State as I expected obliged me to abandon the enterprize for the present and wait to see the result of the New Government that was then forming, with a full determination, when permanently fixed, to make an offer of my service to the State of Virginia, to introduce the Woolen Manufactory on the present most approved plans now working in England and in my own manufactory.' He went on to outline the immense savings in labour brought about by advances in technology, adding a significant remark about the sourcing of labour in America: 'But supposing the number of young white people, that will be requisite for a large Manufactory can not be easily obtain'd I would propose that those Gentlemen who are disposed to emancipate their Negroes would appoint some of their younger ones for that business and give them their freedom after a service of seven years as an Apprentice, then there will be little doubt but they will remain in the business and become useful Members of Society.' He concluded his letter with a suggestion that in exchange for his investment of capital he should be allowed a 'stipend' from the American government to ease the set-up costs he would incur in the early days of the business.

Thomas's American scheme came to nothing, it is sometimes said, because of his natural caution and through lack of support from his wife. Nevertheless, there is something of the pioneering spirit in the Washington letter. His businesses in Hay were closed by the middle of 19th century, unable to compete with the new steam-powered mills in the north. He is buried in Hay churchyard beneath a simple headstone referring to him as 'woolen manufacturer of this town'.

The Victorian era: public spirit

The combination of commercial and religious energy brought with it a spate of construction, effectively resulting in a new town on an old site. Alongside this came a marked improvement in conditions. Health, education and the organised and humane relief of poverty were given priority: sewerage was installed and fresh water wells dug out; Anglicans and Nonconformists founded a cluster of schools catering at one point for 138 children between them; the old Gwynn Almshouses down by Dulas Brook were uninhabitable by the 19th century and new cottages were built by the Harley family in 1832 in Church Street, along with a second block in Brecon Road four years later.

The community at large can take an enormous amount of credit for this boom, though its principal architects were undoubtedly the grandees of the moment: Henry Wellington, the Rev. Humphrey Allen, the Rev. William Latham Bevan and Sir Joseph Bailey. By 1840 gas supplies had been introduced; by 1864 the railway had reached Hay and remained a much-loved feature of local life until it was finally axed by Dr Richard Beeching in the 1960s. The local Fire Brigade was established in 1893; in 1913 Hay residents began to install electricity in their houses.

Hay in modern times

Hay has continued to thrive as a market town, its population consistently hovering around the 1500+ mark. The second-hand book business has, as is well documented, added a remarkable economic layer to the town's life. For the history of the second-hand book trade in Hay, see p. 69.

WILLIAM CAMDEN'S HISTORY OF HAY

William Camden (1551–1623) was born in London and educated at Christ's Hospital, St Paul's School and Oxford University. He was appointed headmaster of Westminster in 1593 and Clarenceux King of Arms in 1597. In his early days at Westminster he spent school holidays travelling in Britain and completed the first ever county by county survey, entitled *Britain, or, a Chorographicall Description of the most flourishing Kingdomes, England, Scotland, and Ireland*.

His description of Hay (unequivocally slanted against Owain Glyndwr) reads as follows:

'And as for Hay, which in British is called Trekethle, that is, The towne in a grove of Hasel trees, in the very utmost skirt of this shire next unto Herefordshire, it standeth hard by the river Wye, well known, as it seemeth, to the Romans, whose coines is often digged up there, and it sheweth also by the ruins that in old time it was walled. But being now as it were decaied it complaineth of that most lewd rebell Owen Glendoweredwy for his furious outrages, who in wasting and spoiling all those countries most villanously did depopulate it and set it on fire.'

His passage on the Silures is a masterpiece of testy 16th-century erudition:

'As for the derivation of that name, I have nothing that sorteth with the nature of the nation. But touching the originall of the people, Tacitus ghesseth by their coloured faces, their countenances, their curled haire, and their situation over against Spaine, that they had their originall from the Spaniards. But Florianus del Campo a Spaniard flatly affirmeth it, who troubleth and toileth himselfe exceedingly to find the Silures in Spaine, and thrusts upon us I know not what of Soloria and Siloria in Biscaie. But to speake of the nature of these Silures, they were a nation very great (for, as we may gather out of Plinie and Tacitus, they seeme to have possessed all South-wales), fierce, valiant, given to war, impatient of servitude, forward to adventure with a resolution (the Romanes call it *pervicacia*), and who would not be brought in either with faire meanes or foule, in all end every of which qualities their posterity have in no point as yet degenerated from ➤

their ancestors. When the Romanes upon an ambitious desire of rule did set upon them, they, trusting to the prowesse and strength of King Caratacus, provoked also and exasperated with a word that Claudius the Emperour let fall, who had said these were so to be destroied, and their name to be extinguished, as the Sugambri had beene rooted out aforetime, annoied the Romanes with so dangerous a warre, by intercepting their bands of auxiliarie forces, by putting to fight that Legion over which Marius Valens was captaine, and by wasting the lands of their Associates, that P. Ostorius, Propraetor of Britaine, being tired with travaile and with the sense of these griefes and troubles, gave up his ghost. Veranius also, governour under Nero, assailed them in vaine. For whereas we read in Tacitus, *illum modicis excursionibus sylvas populatum esse*, that is, *That he made spoile and forraied the woods in small outrodes*, read in lieu of *sylvas*, that is, *woods, Siluras*, that is, *the Silures*, as our friend that most learned Lipsius doth, and you shall read aright. Yet was not this warre husht and finished before the time of Vespasian. For then Julius Frontinus subdued them by force, and kept them under with bands of Legionarie souldiours.'

MAJOR SIGHTS

The major sights of Hay fall for the most part within the 'triangle' referred to in the Introduction, whose points are defined by the sites of the three old medieval gates (marked on the map on pp. 158–59). The three outliers of significance are St Mary's Church, the Norman Motte and Bailey and, further out on the Brecon Road, Hay-on-Wye Cemetery. Since all of these landmarks, even taking into account the outliers, are in easy walking distance of one another, it is possible to visit them all on foot within a full day, half a day if pressed.

Another half day—or full day with a picnic in summer—can be spent exploring Hay's stretch of the Wye Valley Walk, beginning at the Old Black Lion Green and finishing at the Warren. Refreshments can be taken at any time in one of the numerous pubs and restaurants, some of which are of architectural and historical interest. They are covered in the section beginning on p. 123.

A half day and probably much more can be spent in the bookshops of Hay, which are covered in the section beginning on p. 73.

THE NORMAN MOTTE

Hay's first Norman warlord, who can reasonably be claimed as the founding father of the town, was Bernard de Neufmarché (*see p. 17*). It is likely that the Norman motte and bailey near St Mary's church (*map p. 158, A3*) was set up as a reconnaissance post by him and supervised by his deputy, William Revel. It is impossible to appreciate

The Norman motte may not look very formidable today, but in the 12th century it afforded a clear sight-line across the border country.

the strategic importance of the motte from street level, but if one climbs to its summit all becomes clear. The mound affords what would then have been then an uninterrupted view of comings and goings in the valley. Given these advantages, the site would have been a perfect solution pending the construction of the more ambitious fortification, Hay Castle, on higher ground. The bailey is likely to have been a well-fortified wooden construction and there have been various artist's impressions of it, stockade-like in appearance.

The Livestock Market

The bailey stood on what is now the car park and site of the weekly Livestock Market, which takes place every

Thursday in tandem with the lively general market in and around Memorial Square (*see p. 137*). The Livestock Market, an important event in the local calendar, began as a horse and general cattle fair. Today sheep are principally traded. The latest *Farmers Weekly* price records at the time of going to press listed ewes, hoggets (young sheep between about 9 to 18 months) and old season lambs as having been sold at Hay.

TWO BORDER SHEEP BREEDS

Any views a town-dweller might hold on sheep are likely to be unsophisticated. The wider perception is informed by school nativities, readings from the Bible or the occasional and usually ill-judged decision by a primary school to adopt a pet lamb. In the popular mind, one sheep is much the same as another, providing sweaters, Sunday lunch or, failing that, a potent symbol of man's salvation. These views are not shared by owners and breeders of Clun Forest sheep, the hardiest breed in the Welsh Marches, nor of the Kerry Hill breed, true Powys natives originating from the border village of Kerry in Mid Wales.

Were it not borne out by the proven commercial success of Clun Forests, it would be hard to credit the rich yarn of hyperbole that knits together the innumerable virtues of this bold, tan-faced creature. Originating around the mid-1860s, Clun Forests are a mix of Shropshire, Hill Radnor and—importantly—Kerry Hill stock. They are said to be hardy, prolific, obedient, long-lived, fine-muscled, strong-loined and maternal. Their flesh is sweet and their fleece has 'a spinning count of 58 and a high degree of elasticity'. ➤

Group of Kerry Hill sheep, with their distinctive markings.

In 1970 this miracle was introduced into the unforgiving landscape of Novia Scotia, where it has thrived ever since. Kerry Hills are as hardy as Cluns and are especially prized as prolific breeders, having few or no complications with lambing. They are easy to distinguish, with sharply defined black and white faces and fetching white 'ankle socks'.

The transition from basic animal to supersheep took some time to evolve. What the North American Clun Forest Association calls the 'great era of sheep improvement' began in England towards the end of the 18th century. Farmers had begun to realise that meat, as opposed to fleece, was becoming a lucrative commodity. The problem they faced was the time it took for an animal to 'finish', i.e. be ready for market. If this process could be telescoped from four years down to a year then the benefits to turnover would be self-evident. And if such a turnover could be achieved, it had to be sustained by an animal that could breed and forage in harsh conditions and with minimum maintenance. There was much early trial and error, but from the early to mid-19th century, 'quick finishers', ready for market in a year, were consistently bred in Britain. Lamb, in preference to mutton, became the order of the day. Breeders now established 'flock books', recording and monitoring the relative successes of different strains. The Clun quickly became one of the most prized and traded of the new breeds. Sadly, by the end of the '70s, the skies had darkened over the Clun fraternity in Britain. It became increasingly difficult to undercut New Zealand lamb and Clun numbers began to fall. Breeders fought back by crossing their sheep with Leicesters and thereby creating an even quicker finisher, but this was not enough, it seemed, to hold off almost certain disaster. Kerry Hills, meanwhile, reached the critical point of being placed on the Rare Breeds protection list. Today, though, a new dawn breaks. Kerry Hills are no longer considered endangered, and Cluns have fought back. Adapted perfectly to organic farming techniques, they stand doughtily against the Welsh skyline, greeting the new millennium with dark-faced defiance.

ST MARY'S CHURCH

The Parish Church of St Mary, Hay-on-Wye (*map p. 158, A3*) stands on ground that has been occupied by a place of worship since the early 12th century, when the church was appropriated to Brecon Priory. The church collapsed in

about 1700 leaving only the west tower, and the present building was erected in 1833–34 by Edward Haycock Senior, in typical late Georgian 'Churchwarden' Gothic style. The tower is a 15th-century survival, though heavily restored, and the remainder of the church is Haycock's work, with some additions to the chancel made in 1866. This revitalisation, sorely needed after the doldrums into which the Anglican Church in Wales had fallen in the 18th century, was thanks to the Rev. Humphrey Allen, who was appointed curate of Hay in December 1831. Allen, a man of considerable private means, was appalled by the neglect of the church and the effect this had on parish life. The building, he said, was 'dark, comfortless and ill-contrived and quite inadequate in point of size'. Allen and his wife installed themselves in Hay Castle and set about rebuilding the church and working actively towards the welfare of the parish. His achievements included drastically reducing the number of proprietary pews (those rented by prosperous families) and replacing them by 'free' places, this and other innovations being subsidised from his own pocket. He set the scene for further innovations by later incumbents, who included Archdeacon William Latham Bevan, patron of the Hay National School, and the Anglo-Catholic vicar J.J. de Winton, who supported the local Pierrot troupe, driving them around at breakneck speed in a custom-built trailer attached to his motor car. The present incumbent, the Anglo-Catholic Fr Richard Williams, has built on his predecessors' tradition of active ministry and made notable improvements, including the acquisition of the 19th-century blue-and-white Stations of the Cross.

Detail of the carved and gilt case of the 19th-century organ.

Interior of the church

The church interior is wide and spacious, divided into nave and lateral aisles by the arrangement of the pews. A wide organ loft and gallery, attractively supported on slender pillars, extends over the west end and north side. The windows are simple lancets, untraceried, with some glass.

West end: There is a **recumbent effigy**, possibly 14th-century, by the south door. Local legend has it that this is a representation of Maud de St Valery (nicknamed Maud Walbee), the consort of William de Braose, but this is fanciful (*see p. 19 and illustration on p. 20*). Stairs lead up to the organ loft. By far the most dramatic innovation at St Mary's is the installation of a fine **Grade II listed organ**, built in 1883 by Bevington of Soho, London. This instrument, housed in what the Historic Organ Scheme describes as a 'unique case of flamboyant Classical design', belonged originally to John Carbery Evans of Hatley Court in Cambridgeshire. It is well suited to the church acoustics.

Framed drawings hanging here are the original window designs that were never executed (*see below*).

South aisle: At the end of the aisle is a fine **stained-glass window (1)** by Arthur Dix of London, depicting Abraham and Isaac (1906). The framed drawings at the west end are the original Dix designs for two other windows on the south side.

The octagonal alabaster **pulpit (2)** of 1879 is in the style of Nicola and Giovanni Pisano's 13th–14th-century pulpits at Pisa and Siena. The pedestal is surrounded by eight

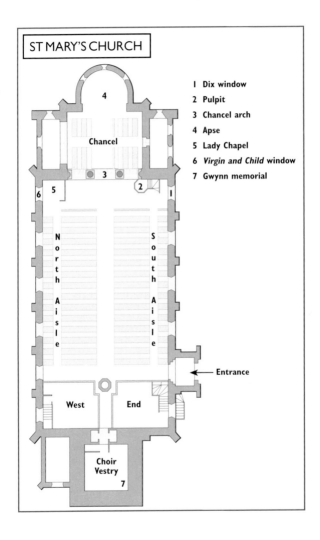

ST MARY'S CHURCH

4

Chancel

3

5

6

2

1

North Aisle

South Aisle

Entrance →

West   End

Choir Vestry

7

1 Dix window
2 Pulpit
3 Chancel arch
4 Apse
5 Lady Chapel
6 *Virgin and Child* window
7 Gwynn memorial

colonnettes and has half-length figures of Christ and the four Evangelists.

East end: Above the **chancel arch (3)** are a number of carved heads. The modern Rood (by local artist Maggie Denny) shows the crucified Christ flanked by the Virgin and St John. The **apse (4)** is decorated by local restorer Georgina Wright. Its conch now bears an image of *Christ Pantocrator* against a rich blue ground decorated with stars in gold leaf.

North aisle: The charcoal drawing of the Virgin in the **Lady Chapel (5)** was made by Janice Armstrong. Also here is a moving memorial to soldiers killed in both World Wars. The fallen of 1914–18 are recorded in faded ink, noting their name, the date, and where they were killed. The stained-glass **window of the *Virgin and Child* (6)** dates from 1945.

Choir Vestry: On the wall here is a memorial to Elizabeth Gwynn (d. 1702) **(7)**, whose family were lords of the manor of Hay for most of the 17th century. She built several almshouses in the town.

The churchyard

The **churchyard** contains some fine examples of Welsh provincial monumental masonry and lettering. Several fallen slabs have been used to pave the walkway on the north side, where there are tablets commemorating members of the Wellington family, who for a time owned Hay Castle.

Turning right out of the churchyard and about 50 yards further on the opposite side of the road, is the site of the Hay Poor Law Union in Union Mews, the **workhouse**, a low Classical building of 1837.

Tombstone of 1840 in St Mary's churchyard, of local workmanship in the Classical style.

HAY CASTLE

Despite the pleasing myth that it was built in a single night by Maud de St Valery (*see p. 19*), Hay Castle (*map p. 158, B2*)clearly grew as a patchwork of heterogeneous additions and repairs as and when its turbulent history dictated. To sum up its history is difficult, but what emerges from Geoffrey Fairs's definitive account is that the history and ownership of the Castle and the Lordship of Hay are best thought of as representing a slow and often troubled transition from a martial to a commercial way of life. Milestones in the castle's history are conveniently marked by the fate and fortunes of its successive owners. The martial period spans the time from the starving to death of Maud de St Valery by King John to the hanging of the 3rd Duke of

Buckingham by Henry VIII in 1521. Thereafter, the high drama of revenge and treason give way to a less turbulent era. The Boyles, Gwynns, Wellingtons, Glanusks and a Guinness lived comparatively uneventful lives at Hay Castle, as for a time did the clergy of the Church in Wales, notably the Rev. Henry Allen, Archdeacon William Latham Bevan and the Rev. J.J. de Winton, who transformed it into what must have been the most striking vicarage in the diocese. It is interesting to note the patrician ease and sense of entitlement that characterised Allen's and then Bevan's incumbency and occupation of the Castle. There are some telling photographs of Bevan in Eric Pugh's *Old Hay in Pictures and Prints*, which clearly show a man at ease in his surroundings and not afraid to exploit the dominance of the Castle as a means of causing change (often for the better) in the town.

Today the Castle is owned by Richard Booth and is the stronghold of his book-dealing enterprises.

Architecture of the Castle

In the early 1230s, Henry III rebuilt the Norman castle and refaced the **main gateway**, still an impressive structure today, with its original medieval timber doors. There are two arches, an inner and an outer, shallow and segmental, and in between these is the portcullis shaft, where the portcullis would have been raised and lowered from a chamber at the high point of the curtain wall walk. This platform is accessible (*not to the general public*) by a small stairway that has passed into local lore. It was up this stairway, during one of Richard Booth's parties in the 1970s, that the author and opera producer Hugh Vickers climbed, a glass of wine in one hand and a bottle in the other. Swaying briefly

THE NORTH ELEVATION OF HAY CASTLE

against the skyline, he lost his footing and plummeted down into the shaft, saved only by his considerable girth, which caused him to be jammed a short way into the crevasse. After much discussion by the local Fire Brigade, he was rescued by a passing potholer.

The Castle preserves interesting later features, no doubt the result of running repairs, such as the pairs of Early Tudor windows in the tower. The most striking juxtaposition, softened by curtains of ivy and unified by evidence of fire damage, is that of the original **Norman keep** with the later **Jacobean mansion** begun for James Boyle of Hereford in about 1660. As early prints testify, this was a handsome, stone-built mansion and something of its dash remains, despite the fires of 1939 (when a magnificent Early Jacobean fireplace was destroyed) and 1977. The tall moulded brick chimneys are a striking feature, as is the 17th-century gateway with is rusticated gate piers and balls, reminiscent of those at Old Gwernyfed, the great Jacobean set piece near Felindre. When the Duke of Beaufort passed through Hay in 1684, he brought with him the artist Thomas Dineley, who made a series of sketches of places they visited. These show the Castle in its heyday, with the Norman stronghold and Jacobean addition intact and with terraces of formal gardens arranged on the slopes leading down to High Town.

Visiting the Castle

A small entrance on Castle Street, opposite the HSBC bank, leads to the inner courtyard with the **Honesty Bookshop**. From here a flight of massive stone steps ascends. There is no access to the main rooms, but on the ground floor is Richard Booth's **Hay Castle Books**, whose interior gives something of the flavour of past domestic elegance from the 17th century onwards.

George Psalmanazar (1679–1763)

For a time in the 18th century, following the death of Elizabeth Gwynn, Hay Castle was split into apartments, one of which was rented by the hoaxer George Psalmanazar.

Psalmanazar had arrived in England in 1703, masquerading as a Formosan scholar, under the protection of the Scottish missionary and army chaplain William Innes. Innes, who was clearly complicit, presented him to the Bishop of London. The story, which won over the bishop and made Psalmanazar the darling of Protestant high society, was that he had been kidnapped by the Jesuits and forced to leave Formosa (modern Taiwan) for Holland. That the 'Formosan' scholar had blond hair, fair skin and a slight Dutch accent made no difference to his enthralled audience. All this could be explained: the Formosan nobility stayed indoors to spare their delicate skins; and George soon crowned his social triumphs with a literary masterpiece, *An Historical and Geographical Description of Formosa.*

The wild claims of the book were greeted as gospel. In Formosa men went naked except for a gold or silver plate to cover their privates. They dined on serpents. Husbands had a right to eat their wives for infidelity. Murderers were hung upside down and shot full of arrows. Every year 18,000 young boys were sacrificed to the gods, the hearts grilled on a gigantic gridiron, the bodies eaten by priests. They lived underground in circular houses. Or, failing that, in large floating villages rowed about by slaves. He invented a language for Formosa and was appointed by Oxford University to translate Christian texts into his native tongue: 'Amy Pornio dan chin Ornio vicy, Gnayjorhe sai Lory, Eyfodere sai Bagalin, jorhe sai domion apo chin Ornio…' began his creditable stab at the Lord's Prayer.

By 1706, though, the strain of deception had become unbearable and Psalmanazar came clean. He spent the rest of his life working as a literary drudge in Grub Street, where his calm, genial, dignified demeanour won him many friends. Samuel Johnson said that 'he had never seen the life of any one that he wished so much his own to resemble'. In later confessions Psalmanazar revealed the secret of the successful hoaxer: 'There was one maxim which I could never be prevailed upon to depart from, viz. that whatever I had once affirmed in conversation, tho' to ever so few people, and tho' ever so improbable, or even absurd, should never be amended or contradicted.' In other words, stick to your story. Psalmanazar died in poverty in London aged 84.

The Castle's cluster of **outbuildings**, linked eventually to Oxford Street by a series of little walkways and lanes, have a decidedly medieval feel: today's shopkeepers and craftsmen (book-dealers, a vintage boutique, cafés, a stonemason) huddle against the Castle walls for shelter and protection much as they would have done in the 14th century. This clustering dependency close to the walls is echoed throughout the town, whose layout has not changed significantly since the Middle Ages.

A closer look at the **main gateway** can be had by turning left at the summit of the steps and skirting the perimeter of the Castle until you find yourself on the large lawn that spreads out in front of the south elevation (*admission 50p; tickets from the bookshop*).

Major restoration work on the Castle was undertaken in 1910 by the distinguished firm W.D. Caroe, coincidentally the employers, for a time, of the artist Eric Gill, who settled at Capel-y-Ffin (*see p. 101*).

AROUND MEMORIAL SQUARE

The Butter Market
Near to the Castle, on High Town, is one of Hay's more striking secular landmarks, the Butter Market (*map p. 159, C2*). This memorable building, reminiscent of a Doric temple, was completed in 1833 by the Quaker William Enoch, a prosperous local trader. It constitutes Hay's contribution to the Greek Revival in Wales and spurred on Sir Joseph Bailey (1st Baronet, English ironmaster and Lord of the Manor of Hay) to complete the Cheese Market two years later (*see below*). The Butter Market serves now, as it did

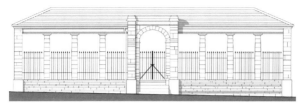

THE BUTTER MARKET

when it was first built, as a covered area for the use of local market traders and farmers. It was used as a food store in the Second World War, primarily as an 'egg station', and was temporarily secured for this purpose by brick walls all around it, now dismantled.

Enclosed by spear-top iron railings, the Butter Market has a timber and slate hipped roof supported by king-post trusses on the open colonnades. The columns have quite a pronounced entasis given the comparatively small scale of the building. In a strange way the lack of theoretical perfection is in fact a pleasing idiosyncrasy, something rather more than mere provincial charm. A plaque on the south side commemorates a recent restoration: 'This building was restored by members of the Warren Club in the year 1984 and opened by Mr Bert Breeze BEM'. The Warren Club won a Prince of Wales Award for this restoration project and continues to be active in local conservation.

The Cheese Market

The Cheese Market (*map p. 159, C2*) is a two-storey building (completed in 1845) that for many years housed the chambers of the Town Council and also served as a meeting place for religious groups, for example that of the Rev.

David Griffiths, who eventually moved his congregation to the Ebenezer United Reformed Church (now the Globe Gallery; *see p. 128*). High on the end wall is a full-length modern statue of Henry VII made by Edward Folkard and given to Hay by a local businessman, Steve Felgate. The Cheese Market's simple, Classical two-storey structure stands on the probable site of the old 17th-century market house. The interior has a broad oak staircase.

Memorial Square

Standing with your back to the Cheese Market and looking upwards, you see the striking historical mish-mash of ruin and make-do-and-mend functionality that constitutes the north elevation of Hay Castle. The space between the market building and the Castle is used as a car park on most days of the week, though it is properly known as Memorial Square, from the **War Memorial** at its south end. This lists men from Hay and Cusop who lost their lives in the two World Wars. Of particular poignance is the fate of four men from the so-called Brecknock Battalion, the 24th Regiment South Wales Borderers. They were a territorial battalion (D Company was based in Hay) and as such had not signed up for active service overseas. But when the time came in 1914 they were eager for adventure and prepared to take their chances. So the Brecknocks, under the command of Colonel Glanusk and with the blessing of their chaplain, Archdeacon Bevan, set off not for France but for Aden, then a British coal station and under threat from the Turkish army. Conditions in Aden were no less horrific than they were in France; there seems to have been a failure by Staff to anticipate the intense heat to which the young men would be subjected, and many Brecknocks died of heat exhaustion. Their sad and absorbing story has been extensively researched by local historian Tim Pugh and can also be traced at the South Wales Borderers Museum in Brecon and on its website.

During the incumbency of Archdeacon Bevan, Memorial Square was an open field, a somewhat cramped equivalent of a village green at the foot of the castle. Bevan and his family, who lived at Hay Castle, were keen toxophilites and encouraged a local revival of archery. Butts were erected on the green and in time there was something of a craze.

Following centuries-old practice, the lively Hay-on-Wye Thursday Market takes place in and around the Butter Market, the Cheese Market and in Memorial Square (*for more on the market, see p. 137*).

THE CLOCK TOWER

The Tump, *twmpa* in Welsh, meaning a 'lump', where Pope Pius IX and Cardinal Wiseman were burnt in effigy in 1850 (*see pp. 65–66*), is now occupied by The Clock Tower (*map p. 158, B2*). A convenient and readily identifiable meeting place, the Clock Tower is an insistent example of High Victorian Gothic. It was also status symbol, as revealed by the remarks of Richard Haslam in the Powys volume of *The Buildings of Wales* (ed. Pevsner), where such towers are described as the 'indispensable if now unfashionable focus of Mid Wales towns'.

Hay's Clock Tower was completed in 1884 to a design by J.C. Haddon of Hereford. A certain Captain Brown, a local man, had left a legacy of £50 specifically for the installation of a clock on the church tower. His executors, mindful of

the shortage of public space in Hay and noting also that the church tower was hardly visible from the centre of town, decided to put the legacy towards a new town clock, a public hall and a corn exchange. This project, intended to burgeon into a major extravaganza of off-the-peg Gothic, foundered through lack of support and only the Clock Tower was built, at a cost of £600. It is an entertaining structure, with much detail, including an open bellcote and a weathervane. It remains the traditional gathering point of the Golden Valley Hunt's Boxing Day Meet, though the Hunt's activities are much curtailed by recent legislation. The transsexual Hay resident April Ashley was photographed standing by the Tower along with the caption 'If I can change, why can't Hay?'.

The clock does not strike

THE CLOCK TOWER

at night: according to Cyril Marwood (*Wisps of Hay*, 1962), the night strike was discontinued because of complaints from Birmingham travelling salesmen staying at Kilvert's about the terrible 'donks' on the quarter, all through the night. When the 'Hay Poisoner', local solicitor Major Herbert Rowse Armstrong (*see box below*), first came under suspicion, the Tower served as a hide for the local constabulary, who crouched behind its machicolations, carefully noting the frequency with which the Major walked across town to buy arsenic 'for his dandelions'.

Herbert Rowse Armstrong (1870–1922)

To many people who knew him, one of the most striking characteristics of the 'Hay Poisoner' was his diminutive stature. He was scarcely more than five feet tall. A keen and accomplished dancer, he could often be seen at Hay functions, nimbly steering a much taller partner to and fro across the floor. He was as light as a feather and his drop, we are told, was one of the longest ever calculated by his hangman, John Ellis. The story of his arrest, trial and execution is well known. Armstrong was a solicitor practising in Hay and a retired Territorial Army officer. A respected man—he was a member of the local Masonic Lodge, read the lesson in church and so on—he was perhaps the last person one might suspect of murdering his wife. True, Mrs Armstrong had been unusually domineering, and it was common knowledge that she had imposed a repressive domestic regime: she rebuked Herbert in public for keeping the servants waiting, forbade him alcohol, called him away from dances because it was 'bath night'. Yet despite all this they were both well respected in Hay ➤

and the idiosyncrasies of their marriage were seen as little more than a welcome diversion from the daily round of provincial life.

Katherine Armstrong died in 1921 from heart disease, it was initially thought, and associated complications. Dr Thomas Hincks, the local doctor, issued the death certificate. Those who gave it any thought reckoned that Armstrong had dutifully nursed his wife throughout her illness, that her death was a blow for him and for their children. All of a sudden, though, events took a dramatic and unexpected turn.

For some time Armstrong had been engaged in a tussle with a rival solicitor, Oswald Martin. Martin had been pressing Armstrong for settlement of a property transaction, and Armstrong invited Martin to tea in an attempt, it was presumed, at reconciliation, passing him a scone with the memorable genteelism, 'Excuse fingers!'. Martin fell ill and during the course of his treatment Dr Hincks became struck by the similarities between Martin's symptoms and those endured by Mrs Armstrong in the last days of her illness. Hincks made his concerns known to the Home Office, who put Armstrong under surveillance: the police noted the regularity with which Armstrong purchased weedkiller (arsenic): to keep the dandelions at bay, he later claimed. Mrs Armstrong was exhumed; the great pathologist Sir Bernard Spilsbury found a damning quantity of arsenic.

Armstrong was arrested on 22nd January 1922 and appointed fellow Cambridge man Sir Henry Curtis-Bennett to represent him. 'Cambridge always win!' said Armstrong, with notable hubris—and so they did, by four-and-a-half lengths in the University Boat Race on the day before the trial started. Armstrong, once spare cox for the University Eight, faced rough waters, made all the more turbulent by Mr Justice Darling, who kept him on the stand and asked all the more awkward questions that the Prosecution had failed to ask. He was found guilty and hanged in Gloucester Prison on 31st May, calmly protesting his innocence to the end. 'I'm coming, Katie!' were Armstrong's last words, an unsettling reminder of summonses home from the dance on bath night. Dr Hincks had exchanged contracts on his practice in Hay, ready for a getaway in the event of an acquittal. He tore them up in relief when news of the verdict came through. The Armstrong children, who remembered an affectionate father, had their name changed and were taken care of by an aunt.

THE GUILD CHAPEL OF ST JOHN

Supervised by the Vicar and under the jurisdiction of the Church in Wales is the Guild Chapel of St John the Baptist in Lion Street (*map p. 159, C2*). Known locally for centuries as 'Church Evan', 'Church Ifan' or in Welsh 'Eglwys Ifan', this is a small Anglican foundation dating from the mid-13th century. It is referred to in a local Survey of Chantries overseen by the Bishop of Llandaf in 1545–46: 'Saint John Chappell ys distant from the Parish Church two flights shootes'. In the pointed arch bellcote there is a bell inscribed 'Edward Wellington CW 1718', made by Henry Williams, the noted bell-founder of Glasbury.

Interior of the chapel

The chapel has a carved Jacobean reredos of domestic origin from Chipford and an oak altar from Whitney. There is a striking and attractive portrait sculpture in the style of Donatello, signed B. Wilson, Florence 1898.

History of the chapel and its dissenters

Church Evan's early history as a chantry and as a chapel for the local Guild of Tradesmen is sparsely documented but it is clear that it was used by local traders for early-morning services on market days. There are entertaining examples of the varied secular uses to which the building has been put over the years as a butcher's, saddler's, barber's, bank and school. It was reported in the *Brecon County Times* in 1811 that Mr Henry Wellington, 'who was a kind of king in Hay and did exactly as he liked, got possession of the belfry and transformed it into a lock-up', which it remained until 1875, when a more fit-for-purpose gaol and court-house were built in Heol y dwr. The first customers of the St John's lock-up were mainly drunken labourers—there were many—drafted in during the Napoleonic Wars to build the first horse-drawn railway, completed in 1816, connecting Hay to the Welsh coalfields. John Wesley records in his journal that he preached here 'within the walls of the old church' on 15th August 1774; and in a historical sense, perhaps, this was the little chapel's finest hour. Wesley's open-air sermon (the roof of Church Evan had collapsed in 1700) was well received and during his stay at Hay Wesley had time to record first-hand accounts by locals of religious life in the town. He learned of the 'Jumpers', the Welsh Calvinistic Methodists, so nicknamed because they jumped for joy at their meetings (*see box on p.*

62), and though delighted by the extent to which Nonconformism had taken root in Wales, he became increasingly perturbed by the activities of extremists.

The stoning of William Seward

Sometimes the activities of extremist Nonconformists had tragic consequences, as happened at Black Lion Green in 1742. This is the site, adjacent to the Old Black Lion pub (*map p. 159, D2*), where the itinerant Methodist preacher William Seward was reputedly stoned to death. Most accounts, one of which is reproduced here, confirm that he died of his injuries shortly after being attacked by a mob of angry locals.

Attacks on itinerant Methodist preachers, or at least serious disruptions of their meetings, were not unusual. Calvinistic Methodists like Seward were regarded as kill-joys by many people in Wales, who heard with resentment a series of eloquent attacks on long-held local customs such as fairs and wakes, annual merrymaking events at which locals let off steam in a round of feasting, dancing and drinking. As for the gentry, they hated the sheer enthusiasm of the itinerant Methodist evangelists, 'a horrid thing' according to Bishop Butler. There are many recorded instances of the imaginative ways in which preaching was disrupted, often with the tacit support of the local clergy and magistrate: preachers were regularly stoned, hurled into rivers and ponds, pelted with rotten vegetables or burnt in effigy. John Wesley himself saw the dangers inherent in unleashing too extreme a flavour of evangelism in Wales. He was annoyed by the more inflammatory remarks contained in William Seward's *Preface*, a document that succeeded in annoying Methodists and non-Methodists

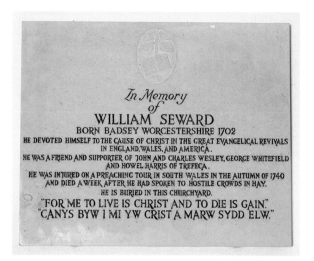

In Memory of
WILLIAM SEWARD
BORN BADSEY WORCESTERSHIRE 1702
HE DEVOTED HIMSELF TO THE CAUSE OF CHRIST IN THE GREAT EVANGELICAL REVIVALS
IN ENGLAND, WALES, AND AMERICA.
HE WAS A FRIEND AND SUPPORTER OF JOHN AND CHARLES WESLEY, GEORGE WHITEFIELD
AND HOWEL HARRIS OF TREFECA.
HE WAS INJURED ON A PREACHING TOUR IN SOUTH WALES IN THE AUTUMN OF 1740
AND DIED A WEEK AFTER HE HAD SPOKEN TO HOSTILE CROWDS IN HAY.
HE IS BURIED IN THIS CHURCHYARD.
"FOR ME TO LIVE IS CHRIST AND TO DIE IS GAIN."
"CANYS BYW I MI YW CRIST A MARW SYDD ELW."

Memorial to William Seward in Cusop church, on the English side of
Dulas Brook. Seward lies buried in the graveyard.

alike. Wesley himself had been prompted to reflect on the
possible benefits of moderate homiletics after a notable
occasion on which he attempted to reform a gathering of
drunks in Cardiff, pointing out that if you were a drunkard,
then a place in Hell had surely been reserved for you. 'I am
one, and Thither I goe!' came the defiant rejoinder of one
of the merrymakers, typifying the resistance that any itinerant preacher would be likely to meet in Wales.

The following is an anonymous account of Seward's
stoning and death:

'It was in the autumn of the year 1742, that a gentleman
from Badsey, in Worcestershire, Seward by name, passed

through the town of Hay in his journey to a place in the interior of Wales. The town at that time was noted for wickedness, and the great spiritual darkness of the people. If tradition speaks truly, Mr Seward was a man full of the Holy Ghost and of faith. Pitying the ignorance of the people, he resolved before he left to preach to them the Word of Life. At one end of the town is an open plain or "Green", which is interesting as the spot where he stood up to address the people. It now bears the name of "Black Lion Green". Above is a portion of the old town wall, and below runs the little brook which divides the counties of Hereford and Brecon. Making it known that he was about to preach on the Green, the man of God stood up with the love of Christ in his heart, and a message of gladness on his tongue. For a while he was listened to in silence by the wondering people; but before his discourse was ended, Satan began to rage in earnest. Some of the most reprobate among the inhabitants, raising a disturbance, began rudely to assault the preacher. Stones were cast at him, and several of the bystanders were injured. One cowardly ruffian, standing behind the preacher, threw at him a huge stone, which, striking his head, caused him to fall senseless to the ground. He was carried to the inn at which he had been staying, and there died from the effects of the blow. Whether he died shortly after or lingered some days in pain is not now known; but it is said that with his last breath he forgave his murderer, and requested that no efforts should be made to punish him. The man who hurled the fatal missile was well known, and lived for many years after. But he lived and died unchanged, and his deathbed was attended with peculiar horrors, and, in the words of one who witnessed it, "the room seemed full of devils".'

ENGLISH RESERVE VERSUS WELSH JUMPING

'Some of them leaped up many times, men and women, several feet from the ground; they clapped their hands with the utmost violence; they shook their heads; they distorted all their features; they threw their arms and legs to and fro, in all variety of postures; they sang, roared, shouted, screamed with all their might, to the no small terror of those that were near them. One gentlewoman told me she had not been herself since, and did not know when she should. Meantime the person of the house [the Calvinist minister in charge] was delighted above measure, and said, "Now the power of God is come indeed".'

So wrote John Wesley (*Journal, 6:37*) of the 'Jumpers', a derogatory English term for the branch of the Welsh Calvinistic Methodists whom he encountered when he preached at the Guild Chapel of St John the Baptist in Hay. The English clergyman William Bingley was dismayed by their antics, which resembled those of the so-called 'Convulsionists', French Protestant exiles who settled in and around Wales. Bingley encountered Jumpers at Carnarvon: 'The noise of their groaning and singing, or oftentimes rather bellowing, the clapping of their hands, the beating of their feet against the ground, the excessive heat of the place, and the various motions on all sides of me, almost stupefied my senses. The less enthusiastic move off soon after the hymn is begun; among these, every time I attended them, I observed the preacher to make one [of the various motions]; he always threw a silk handkerchief over his head, and, descending from the pulpit, left his congregation to jump by themselves.'

The great Welsh preacher Christmas Evans (1766–1838), by contrast, was a vigorous defender of the Jumpers and a critic of English *sang froid* which, he thought, stifled the word of God. The English would rather hear an eloquent barrister than a good preacher: 'The burying grounds are kept in fine order in Glamorganshire, and green shrubs, and herbs grow on the graves; but all this is of little value, for the inhabitants of them are all dead. So, in every form of godliness, where its power is not felt, order without life is exceedingly worthless: you exhibit all the character of human nature, leaving every bud of the flower to open in the beams of the sun, except in Divine worship. On other occasions, you English appear to have as much fire in your affections as the Welsh have, if you are noticed. In a court of law, the most efficient advocate, such as Erskine, will give to you the greatest satisfaction; but you are contented with a preacher speaking so lifelessly, and so low, that you can hardly understand a third part of what he says, and you will call this decency in the sanctuary...' The Welsh Jumper, on the other hand, 'creates the channel where the living waters flow, and dead fish are made alive by its virtues'.

The definitive texts on jumping were written by its greatest defender, the Welsh hymn-writer William Williams Pantycelyn (1717–91), part of whose studies had been accomplished near Hay at Llanigon. His *Llythyr Martha Philopur at y Parchedig Philo Evangelius eu hathro* (*Martha Philopur's letter to the Reverend Philo Evangelius her teacher*) and its sequel *Atteb Philo-Evangelius i Martha Philopur* (*Philo-Evangelius's reply to Martha Philopur*) describe the techniques and benefits of jumping.

THE CEMETERY

Hay-on-Wye Cemetery, a short walk down Church Street and the Brecon Road after the Swan Hotel, was built in 1870 as an expansion of the churchyard. It is well tended and contains numerous well-preserved headstones dating back to the 17th century, removed from the churchyard for preservation. Here, as in churchyards and cemeteries elsewhere in this part of the country, one is struck by the quality of the memorials. Glovers, carpenters, lace-makers and other comparatively minor tradespeople are commemorated with lavish headstones and monuments that in London would have been associated only with the gentry.

A tour of the cemetery

At the cemetery entrance is a fine timber and slate **lych gate**, dedicated to the memory of Archdeacon William Latham Bevan and presented by members of his family. Nearby is an imposing sundial. The first plot, to the left of the central avenue, is the resting place of a group of **German and Italian servicemen**, who died here as prisoners of war. Fifty yards further on, again to the left of the central avenue, is a fine Celtic cross, the **memorial of Archdeacon Bevan**.

The most absorbing memorial in the cemetery is a masterpiece of funerary art: the **grave of Pilot Officer Lancelot Steele Dixon** of the RAF, who was killed when his Hurricane crashed at Winterton, near his family home, on 9th April 1940. 'Lanty' Dixon, as he was known, was the son of the sculptor Christine Goad by her first marriage. She subsequently married the novelist Rafael Sabatini, who grew to love Lanty, his own son Rafael-Angelo having been killed in a car crash in 1927. An exultant Lanty flew over the family home at Winterton the day he received his RAF wings. He performed increasingly dangerous aerobatics until he finally lost control of his aircraft. It crashed near the house and burst into flames. In the memorial, made by his mother, Lanty is depicted life-size as the fallen Icarus. His recumbent form gives the powerful and unsettling feeling that he is merely sleeping and might be awoken by the gentlest touch on the bare shoulder or the feathered wing. There is a brief inscription, *Mater Luctuosa Fecit*: 'made by a sorrowful mother'.

ST JOSEPH'S

St Joseph's Catholic Church in Belmont Road (*map p. 158, B2*) is the present home of the Roman Catholic congregation in Hay.

History of Catholics in Hay

Roman Catholics were was not formally established here until 1926, when John Grant of Hay obtained permission from the Bishop of Menevia to hold services in rooms above the Town Hall. Up until then there had been only a few references to Catholics in Hay. For example, one Roger Harper of Hay, an innkeeper, is reported in the records of the St David's diocese in 1706 as a 'suspected papist'.

It was not until the 19th century that there was any serious outburst of anti-Roman feeling in Hay, the most notable being that of Guy Fawkes' Night 1850, when the citizens assembled at The Tump, now the site of the Clock Tower, and burnt effigies of Pope Pius IX and Nicholas, Cardinal

Wiseman. This flare-up was occasioned by the recent pub-
lication of the Bull *Universalis Ecclesiae*, by which Pius IX
sought to establish a Roman Catholic bishopric in Britain,
his intention being to emancipate the Roman Catholic
Church from the 'underground' status it had endured since
the death of its last Marian bishop in 1688. The Bull was
widely seen as an arrogant attempt by the Pope and his
henchman the Cardinal to 'Romanise' Britain: Cardinal
Wiseman's ill-judged *Pastoral Letter*, the follow-up to
Universalis Ecclesiae, was a document disastrously open to
misinterpretation. Its readers felt, wrongly but widely, that
the Bull would give the Pope temporal as well as spiritual
power in Britain and that as a result Roman Catholics
would be in a position to exercise control over everyone
else—a situation that would not have gained ready accept-
ance anywhere in Britain, let alone the Welsh Marches.

The next anti-Rome incident came over a hundred years
later, in 1968, when the congregation acquired its present
place of worship. This time the problem was occasioned by
what many saw as an almost heretical severance with tradition. For St Joseph's occupies the former Calvinistic
Methodist Tabernacle, home of the spiritual descendants of
the 'Jumpers' (*see p. 62*). When the Roman Catholic Church
bought the building, it inevitably provoked outcry in certain quarters. Notable Protestants, including the Rev. Ian
Paisley, were dismayed, and phrases such as 'Whore of
Babylon' were given both whispered and stentorian utter-
ance in the neighbourhood.

The building

The original Methodist Tabernacle was built in 1829 and
the present, more substantial, stone building was com-

pleted in 1873. The striking, colourful stained glass windows, in an abstract design, are recent additions and form a pleasing contrast to the overall austerity of the building.

THE NONCONFORMIST CHAPELS

Of the Nonconformist chapels in Hay, the oldest is the **Salem Chapel** in the Bullring (*map p. 159, C2*), dating to 1649 when the congregation was established by the prominent Baptist John Miles. The original site now houses an art gallery, and the present chapel adjoining it was built in 1814 and remodelled in simple Gothic form in 1878.

Also of interest for its Italianate tower is the **former Trinity Chapel** in Oxford Road, now a private house next to a country supply store to the left of the 17th-century castle gateway. What is now the **Bethesda Evangelical Church** in Oxford Road (*map p. 159, C2*) was built by the Primitive Methodists in 1865, as witnessed by the intricately undercut stone inscription. Constructed in red brick under a slate roof, its Gothic windows have tracery in the decorated style topped with hood moulds. There is a striking little spirelet.

THE KINGDOM OF BOOKS

There is a defining moment in the film *Borderline*, a documentary about Hay revolving around the life and work of Richard Booth. In one scene, Booth is pictured in the back of a lorry unloading the last of yet another bulk purchase of books. He gathers a final armful of volumes and flings them exuberantly into the street, as profligate with books as Mark Antony was with provinces: 'realms and islands were as plates dropp'd from his pocket'. In his Honesty Bookshop outside Hay Castle there is an open-air courtyard lined with bookcases on all sides. Clustering round the Castle walls are open lean-to shacks full of books: if you are honest, you pay and may take them at any hour of the day or night. These volumes sit outdoors throughout the Welsh winter waiting to be bought or stolen. As Booth muses in his autobiography, *My Kingdom of Books*, '…at the end of the summer season the books become like wilting autumn leaves; faded and rain-soaked, they tumble damply from the shelves'.

The life and legacy of Richard Booth

Booth was born in 1938, the son of Colonel Philip Booth of Brynmelin House at nearby Cusop Dingle. He underwent the conventional rites of passage for one of his class: prep school, public school, university. He developed an early interest in books as a result of meeting Edward Fineron, a former Guards officer whose shop in Woking afforded Booth some consolation from the Spartan rigours of public school life. He went up to Oxford with some reluctance and his time at Merton was to some extent enli-

'Blue Plaque' on the Old Fire Station building on Castle Street commemorating Richard Booth's first second-hand bookshop.

vened by the presence of exotic friends including fellow Rugbeian Hugh Vickers (*see p. 46*). As so often happens at Oxford, formative influences were encountered in a totally unexpected quarter. For Booth they were embodied in the flamboyant person of Kyril Bonfiglioli, a former Army sabre champion who ran an antiques shop on Little Clarendon Street. The friendship of the convivial and uninhibited Bonfiglioli, whose premises offered an agreeable mix of pretty girls, wine and books, strengthened Booth's resolve to become a book-dealer. After a listless attempt at accountancy, for which he showed no promise, he set off back to the Black Hill to make his fortune.

He opened his first shop in 1962 in what was then the Old Fire Station in Hay, now the premises of Boz Books. In 1969 he bought the New Plaza Cinema and converted it into a huge bookshop (it is now the Hay Cinema Bookshop, under different ownership). By now his early apprenticeships with Fineron and Bonfiglioli were beginning to pay off and by the end of the '60s he was making a profit of £100,000 a year. He celebrated this by buying himself a Rolls Royce Phantom V, of which a local artist later made a life-size sculptural replica solely out of books. In 1971 he bought Hay Castle and converted part of it into the shop that he still owns. Later he bought the huge former agricultural merchant's at 44 Lion Street, 'The Limited' (see p. 74).

In those days the book trade was still 'wide open', in the sense that there were still massive country-house libraries for sale whose owners were all too happy to clear their dusty shelves for whatever they could get. Lorry-loads of calf folios and incunabula, the centuries-old loot of Grand Tour libertines, could now be picked up for guineas, shillings or the price of a pint. No library was too large to deter Booth, no country house too distant or dilapidated. The first bulk purchase was the library of Bishop Headley, the Catholic Archbishop of York, and from then on there were many more: close to home in Wales; in chill castles on the Scottish borders; in the straitened country houses of Ireland, hidden away in the libraries of the Anglo-Irish gentry, where birds nested and grass could be seen growing through the floor.

The mid-'70s saw a sharpening of Booth's already keen sense of social injustice. Government at a local and national level was, he felt, letting its citizens down. Everywhere seemed either paralysed by the dead hand of bureaucracy or vandalised by a disproportionate haemorrhage of public funds on wasteful projects. No thanks to government, Hay already had a thriving rural economy and was now riding high on the strength of the book-dealers: book buyers came and went in increasing droves, spending money not only in bookshops but also in pubs, hotels and local shops. The time had come to take a stand—and on April Fools' Day

1977 Booth declared Hay an independent kingdom and himself the King. Why plod along *sicut regale* in the old fashion of the Welsh Marches when you could easily declare yourself Rex Imperator? He appointed his horse, Caligula, Prime Minister and appointed as 'consort' April Ashley, Duchess of Hay and Offa's Dyke. The resulting publicity worked wonders for the town and gave Booth a platform from which he offered a shrewd and wounding running commentary on the remorseless desecration of rural Britain by corrupt and unimaginative bureaucrats and businessmen.

Booth received an MBE for services to tourism in the 2004 New Year's Honours List. He announced his retirement in 2005 but actively promotes the concept of booktowns world wide—there are many (*see p. 88*)—and his interest and presence in Hay remain as strong as ever. In September 2009 Peter Harries of Boz Books declared the town a commonwealth. Booth was tried and found guilty of 'no longer fulfilling his duties to his kingdom in terms of publicity'. An effigy of the King of Hay was beheaded but Booth, who attended the ceremony, bit back with the promise of a new campaign, 'The Peasants are Revolting'.

His legacy is phenomenal. The sheer quantity of books in Hay-on-Wye beggars belief. Nobody has a definitive figure, but estimates hover at around ten million volumes, including everything on display and in storage and, as one dealer mysteriously puts it, with 'men in the hills', dealers without fixed premises but who nevertheless operate in the vicinity—in effect the book-dealing equivalent of the mysterious men of Elfael, elusive bandits in the reign of Henry VI. In Hay one encounters in many of the shops a beguiling species of organised chaos wherein books are organised into shelved sections—railways, poetry, Renaissance art and so on—but amongst the shelved sections there are cairns, quarries, warrens of unsorted material. 'A good book', to quote John Milton, 'is the precious life blood of a master spirit, embalmed and treasured up on purpose for a life beyond...', and in Hay there are good, bad and indifferent books on every subject: pottery, satanism, travel, pornography, economics, Morris dancing, incest, cookery; paper covers splashed with lurid '50s dames, bug-eyed dope-fiends, sallow vampires; expert texts on long-case clocks, poodles, Messerschmitts, volcanoes, Temperance Societies; fine bindings tooled with lilies, inset with lapis lazuli; sermons by long-forgotten clergymen, tracts, polemics, manifestos, eulogies; there are confessions, denials, affirmations; love, hate, war, peace, faith; grammar, soufflés, the science of controlled explosion. That there are ten million books in Hay on these and other subjects—and that Hay's book-dealing business goes from strength to strength nearly four decades after the first shop opened in 1962 is all thanks to Richard Booth.

THE DEALERS

The book-dealers in Hay are, with a couple of exceptions, dispersed throughout the small central triangle of the town. All carry a leaflet listing each shop and marking its location on a sketch map of the town.

Bookshops on and around Lion Street

The Sensible Bookshop (*T: 01497 822969*) is sensible because it is small, which makes it a good place to start. The staff will not admonish you for your *outré* tastes in curiosa or your extravagant expenditure on fine bindings. Described accurately by the *Daily Telegraph* as being 'of a tolerable size', it is a good initiation for those daunted by the more cavernous and rambling shops in Hay. There is an excellent basement full of appealing bargains.

The Bookshop (*T: 01497 821341*), on The Pavement (between Lion St and High Town), is a solid and well-stocked generalist, an adept exponent of the 'iceberg' effect, with over 400,000 books in stock in the warehouse at any given time. The bookshop has outlets in Gloucester, Newport and London and holds one-day Hall Sales as far afield as Worcester, Stafford and Caerphilly.

Richard Booth's Bookshop ('The Limited'; *T: 01497 820322*) is the largest bookshop in Hay. Its narrow and elegant façade, decorated with an array of glazed *animalier* tiles, leads

A comfortable seat in Richard Booth's Bookshop.

Stout pig in straw. One of the charming animal tiles decorating the façade of Richard Booth's Bookshop, a former agricultural store.

in to a vast three-floor emporium. The building originally belonged to Robert Williams & Sons, for a time the only Limited Company in Hay, hence the nickname. Williams dealt in agricultural machinery and needed a great deal of space. Inevitably the cavernous interior in those days was often borrowed by the community for dances and other celebrations. Now, fittingly, there are screenings, readings and theatrical performances throughout the year as well as drinks parties, launches and other literary gatherings. There are two cats, a mother and daughter, who can often be seen sitting on the grand staircase or curled up in one of the many sofas placed strategically around the shop. They belong to the new owners, Paul Greatbatch and Elizabeth Haycox, and soon after moving in had successfully cleared the basement of mice. Elizabeth introduced elements of order and luxury into various quarters of the building—there are sumptuous lavatories in the basement—and there is now a lift (it was planned that Richard Booth should be the first passenger). There is an attractively decorated children's section with miniature armchairs, toys and paintings.

Addyman Books (*T: 01497 821136*) is another Hay institution. 'Addyman's upstairs is like a perfect sitting-room, floor to ceiling Modern Firsts.' There are armchairs and sofas, knowledgeable staff, no sense of rush.

Murder and Mayhem (*T: 01497 821613*), the second of three Addyman presences in Hay, founded by Derek Addyman and Anne Brichto to cope with the increasing demand for true crime classics and crime fiction. There is always an agreeably bizarre window display featuring a beguiling and lurid selection of detective fiction, true crime and horror alongside the obligatory discarded syringe, deerstalker and violin. The true crime section is a tiny, very effectively decorated shrine to its subject, offering absorbing titles such as *Cheating at Cards*, *Secrets of a Solicitor* and *Rats and Squealers*. The shop stocks two books about the 'Hay Poisoner' (*see p. 55*): Robin Odell's, which makes out he did it and local solicitor Martin Beales's, which maintains he didn't.

The Poetry Bookshop (*T: 01497 821812*) in the Ice House, Brook St, is the first bookshop in Britain dedicated solely to poetry, and at a refined and all-encompassing level. The scope of the shop is best summed up in the words of a very well-heeled American collector, clearly a former hippie, who was heard discussing his visit while sitting at the bar of Kilvert's Hotel: 'I go in for Beat and I'm like William Burroughs. And he's like, Franco Beltrametti, Black Crackle, Montague Summers. Way out, man.'

The Ice House is so called not as a reference to the 'cool' nature of the Beat section but rather for the interesting 18th-century subterranean food-storage chamber that occupies the foundations of the building. There is some fine lit crit and a selection of hard-to-find and very reasonably priced collections and anthologies.

The Hay Book Company (*T: 01497 821641*) on High Town is an admirable generalist open seven days a week.

Bookshops on Castle Street

Hay-on-Wye Booksellers (*T: 01497 820382*) are semi-specialist dealers in art, photography, design and computer science.

Mostly Maps (*T: 01497 820539*) has rare but surprisingly inexpensive (in the hundreds) works by the 17th-century master John Speed, the tailor-turned-cartographer whose generous patron Sir Fulke Greville found him a job in customs and gave him 'full liberty to express the inclination of my mind'. There are excellent and again reasonably priced souvenirs of the area, including work like Pieter van den Keere's *Radnor, Brecknok, Cardigan and Caermarthen*.

The Wye Gallery (*T: 01497 821163*) stocks signed limited-edition prints by established and emerging artists including Gillian McDonald, Frances St Clair Miller, Donna Crawshaw, Rhian Simes,

Anne Cotterill and Rob Ritchie.

The Addyman Annexe (*T: 01497 821600*), Addyman's third presence in Hay, offers a recherché collection of works on Beat, sex, drugs, art, poetry, philosophy, left-wing history and the occasional occult work. This is Hay's 'jewel in the crown' according to *Antiquarian Book Review*; 'Put me in Addyman's and I lose all reason,' says one of the characters in Sue Gee's *Reading in Bed*. The striking paintings along Castle St were commissioned by Addyman from a local signwriter, John Morgan. The bookish, somewhat reproachful figure in 18th-century rig in one of them (reproduced on the title page of this book) is a self-portrait.

Bookends (*T: 01497 821572*) is an excellent place for the cautious bibliophile, offering attractive books of all kinds, all of which cost £3 or less and look as though they cost a great deal more. Good if you're on a budget or if you are a non-reader who would like to create a wall-to-wall library of classics on a tight budget (*see Wholesalers on p. 84*).

Hay Castle Books (*T: 01497 820503*) is the final stronghold of Richard Booth, up at the Castle. They will arrange 'bulk sales from our warehouse to people wishing to emulate Hay's success in filling empty shops with books'. The interior of the Castle bookshop is stately, the remains of Boyle's Jacobean set-up. There is a pleasing mix of disorder and order and an intriguing and seemingly unsorted section of photograph albums and loose photographs. There are cabinets full of Daguerreotypes of severe aunts, hopeful girls, awkward soldiers, whiskery bigots. Some albums are stripped bare, others contain fascinating topographical views of Cairo or Clyro. A lot of calf in the cabinet, as they say in the trade; some serious works under lock and key in the front section.

Bookshops on Backfold

Backfold Books (*T: 01497 820171; Oxford Rd corner*). A good generalist selling history, poetry, travel, topography, transport, fiction.

Greenways Corner Bookshop (*T: 01497 820443*) stocks a general selection of hardback and paperback fiction and non-fiction.

Bookshops on Broad Street

Oxford House Books (*T: 01497 820191*) is a compact, well-stocked generalist with an emphasis on non-fiction. Good and constantly changing stock including art, history, religion, philosophy, poetry, literary criticism, politics, economics, travel and topography.

Broad Street Book Centre (*T: 01497 821919*). A large and very well-organised emporium showcasing the stock of over a dozen dealers at any given time. Dealers include Matthew Nutt (collectable and antiquarian); Geoff Carss (geology and palaeontology); Chris Luddington (Observer, Ladybird, Shire Albums); Get2Books (European royalty, genealogy, biography); Les Barrett (general, history and maps); Alen Harrison (fiction, crafts, poetry, topography); Mike Hobday (railway, models, relics, ephemera); Stephanie Smith (children's, fiction); Orbiting Books (spirituality, healing, cookery); Matthew Bright (topography, archaeology, natural history); Literary Cat (collectables, antiquarian, prints); Kestrel (modern firsts); Guru Bookshop (Buddhism, Hinduism, spirituality, Oriental religions); Hazel Heightly (Churchill specialist, modern firsts, natural history); Garfi Books (WW2, land, air and sea forces); LTS (children's, general); Tommy Jenkins (stamps and football programmes); Hancock & Monks (classical CDs, DVDs, scores).

Hancock & Monks (*T: 01497 610555*) stock an impressive collection of books on music alongside sheet music, scores, new and used classical CDs and DVDs and audio books. Some of the most arcane recordings can be found here: it was not a problem to locate the ever-elusive Besançon recital by Dinu Lipatti or the original vinyl of Ferenc Fricsay's *Don Giovanni*. There is a solid collection of jazz. The operation is backed up by a strong internet presence.

Hole in the wall for coins at the Honesty Bookshop at Hay Castle.

Rose's Books (*T: 01497 820013*) is a specialist shop dealing in rare and out-of-print children's books with an extensive stock of affordable classics alongside the exquisite first editions. Thus it is possible to acquire an unsullied and very valuable copy of Blyton's *Bimbo and Topsy* or a slightly bumped and crayoned later edition of the same thing for a few pounds. There is a small but glittering cabinet filled with pristine examples of Victorian illustrated books untouched and unspoiled by young hands.

Outcast Books (*T: 01497 821292*). In chill contrast to the nursery atmosphere of Rose's, David Howard trades from a spartan outhouse next door in the courtyard. There is a small, well-stocked general section but the main draw is a constantly revolving stock of key works in the fields of social studies, humanistic psychology, psychotherapy, philosophy and human relations. A solid corpus of important set texts accompanies a good selection of scarce works from the further shores of self-help.

Bookshops on Church Street

Boz Books (*T: 01497 821277*). Come here for fine bindings and immaculate literary sets. Peter Harries has a special interest in 19th-century English literature and stocks a wide selection of Dickens first editions as well as other authors of the period. He is always keen to buy the following in first or good Victorian editions: M.E. Braddon, Mrs Oliphant, Wilkie Collins, George Eliot, Trollope, Rider Haggard and Thomas Hardy. There is an interest in 20th-century work too, notably Dylan Thomas and Mervyn Peake.

Harries is also Hay's leading Republican, and publishes a magazine, *Hay Wired*, in which he mounts a vigorous stand for or against the issue of the month.

C. Arden (*T: 01497 820498*). This is a holy grail of specialist bookshops, even the 'general' sections being more specialist than most specialists could ever hope to be. The principal focus is on bees and bee-keeping but there is a fine selection of natural history, gardening, botany, ornithology and angling. The Arden catalogues themselves are works to relish. We learn that in *My Bee Book* by the Rev. William Charles Cotton the author adopts a 'very moral tone in advocating the use of a puffball narcotic to spare the lives of bees'. However, his rival Mr T. Nutt, author of *Humanity to Honey Bees*, maintains that the same author had 'silently and surreptitiously' filched one

of Nutt's illustrations and included it in one of his own publications. The works on gardening and botany contain beautiful illustrations and it seems that many sales are destined as gifts, once again underlining the persistence of the book as a desirable object.

Hay Cinema Bookshop (*T: 01497 821900*) is a huge converted cinema—note the spangled ceiling and the site of the former projection box —immaculately kept, very well organised, stocking a huge range of books on most subjects. There is a serious antiquarian section and **Francis Edwards** (*T: 01497 820070*), dealers in London since 1855, maintain a solid presence on the first floor. There is a striking metal-clad pyramid in the forecourt with occasional glazed display panels containing books—a Hay landmark and a meeting place, it turns out, for young lovers.

Wholesalers

HCB Wholesale (*T: 01497 820333*) is the wholesale department of Hay Cinema Bookshop with a warehouse in Forest Road Park.

Hay-on-Wye Books (Trade) (*T: 01497 820382*). Another vast wholesale operation, in Gypsy Castle Lane. With regard to wholesale, economists will be fascinated to note that dealers in Hay report a dramatic upsurge in bulk sales to non-readers. These are people who have little or no time to read—they can pull what little information they need from the web—but who value books as objects. To these clients and their decorators, a library is an 'installation', a work of art. And it doubles as an intellectual status symbol because if shrewdly assembled it can create the uncanny impression that it has been read in full by its owner. To be sure, books age in different ways and for different reasons and if your 'new' library looks too heterogeneous then your guests might smell a rat.

Out of Town

The Children's Bookshop (*T: 01497 821083*) is a mile from Hay on the Clifford Road and stocks a large selection of children's literature.

Ashbrook Garage (*T: 01497 821046*) is based at the garage in Clyro and specialises in motoring and motor racing with an added interest in local history.

And finally, where do you go to buy new books? The answer is **Pembertons** on High Town (*T: 01497 821902*), official stockists for the Festival (they run the Book Tent).

THE HAY FESTIVAL

The Drill Hall in Lion Street now serves as the administrative headquarters of the Guardian Hay Festival of Literature and the Arts, one of the most important literary festivals in the world with an impressive international presence: there are sister festivals in Mantua, Segovia, Cartagena, Nairobi, Paraty, Zacatecas, Belfast, Beirut and the Maldives. The smooth metropolitan atmosphere at the Drill Hall today, presided over by the energetic festival organiser Peter Florence, is an aeon away from the days when Captain Arthur Cheese presided over D and H Companies of the 1st Breconshire Volunteer Battalion. Then, the stark, utilitarian building resounded to the bellows of drill instructor Sergeant George Monaghan. Now, one is more likely to hear whispered confirmation of a guest appearance by Judi Dench or the calm negotiation of Jools Holland's availability for the Barcelona gig.

Norman Florence and his son Peter, funded by winnings from a poker game, founded the festival in 1988. The Florences sought to build on Hay's reputation as a booktown. For Peter Florence, 'the idea, then as now, was to celebrate great use and users of language: writers, playwrights, songwriters, screenwriters, comedians, journalists'. In the early days, there was a certain level of resistance. 'Hay-on-Wye, what kind of sandwich is that?' was the somewhat feeble riposte of Arthur Miller when asked to headline the festival in 1989. By 2001, however, another great American swashbuckler, Bill Clinton, had praised the festival unreservedly as 'the Woodstock of the mind', leaving the following year's guest, Jimmy Carter, a hard act to follow. Now firmly established in the nation's cultural calendar, drawing nearly

100,000 visitors every year, the Hay Festival attracts leading writers, ideologues, politicians and celebrities of all kinds. Ted Hughes read his last collection of poetry here, *Birthday Letters*, the harrowing account of his marriage to Sylvia Plath. The reading took place, appropriately, during a thunderstorm, and flashes of lightning lit up the Laureate's monolithic features. A culture-randy heckler publicly propositioned Harold Pinter; Tony Curtis recited his graphic account of affairs with Marilyn Monroe and Joan Collins; William Golding went sleepwalking in a cap and nightgown. Star turns have included Jeremy Paxman, Desmond Tutu, Stephen Fry, Hanif Kureishi, Sandi Toksvig, Danny Quah, David Frost, Rowan Williams and Rowan Atkinson. It is said locally that Andy McNab and Salman Rushdie take care of one another in a hideout in the Black Mountains.

The festival has achieved national recognition for its role in re-energising the local economy in the form of a Queen's Award for Enterprise in 2009, which neatly complements Richard Booth's MBE for Services to Tourism. There is a great deal of outreach in evidence in addition to the international sister festivals already mentioned. Hay has taken over the formerly ailing Brecon Jazz Festival; Hay Fever is a festival event aimed primarily at children and their families; there are exhibitions, workshops, musical events, screenings, political debates and writing masterclasses. One-off events in London and elsewhere throughout the year, organised by HF, have included talks by Margaret Atwood, Michael Palin, Harold Evans and Anthony Horowitz.

A telling observation made by Peter Florence and borne out by conversations with locals is that as a result of the Hay Festival and the book trade, a good proportion of children and teenagers regard 'culture' as a natural condition of

The Pyramids recreated in a Welsh field. Three Festival marquees.

life rather than as an occasional 'add-on' to be endured or avoided. If this is the consequence of the endeavours of Florence, Booth, Lawson, Morelli and others, then their idiosyncratic attitude might be one that other towns would do well to emulate, even on a small scale.

The Festival site and transport from Hay

The Festival site is a large field a little way out of Hay, a move made necessary by the event's dramatic expansion over the last decade. There are shuttle buses, sponsored by local businesses, ferrying visitors to and from the site at regular intervals (they leave from Hay-on-Wye car park and Clock Tower). This was a welcome innovation, since there is a great deal going on in Hay during the Festival. It is a good idea to book accommodation in Hay itself, so as not to miss out on events taking place in the town centre.

For all festival details, see www.hayfestival.com. Festival Box Office: T: 01497 821299.

BOOKTOWNS

Hay is twinned with two markedly different towns, Redu in Belgium and Timbuktu in Mali. Timbuktu is the more recent alliance, made in 2007, underlining the fact that it is not, as many people think, some semi-mythical location. Following the building, in the 15th century, of a number of mosques and madrasahs, it gradually accumulated one of the finest collections of scholarly manuscripts in existence. The Ahmad Baba Institute, where many of these are now preserved (thanks to the support of Bill Gates and others), is named after the 16th-century West African historian Ahmad Baba al-Massufi al-Tinbukti.

Redu is a rather different place, an attractive town in the Ardennes that has, since 1984, steadily grown into a booktown along Hay lines. This is thanks to former oil executive Noël Anselot, who struck up a friendship with Richard Booth in the late '70s. Anselot, who had bought a substantial property in Redu and was a keen book collector, saw the potential in Booth's booktown blueprint and applied it to Redu. It would be possible, he felt, to stimulate the local economy without in any way corroding the considerable charm of the location.

Booktowns now have their own international association and the concept is spreading throughout the world. In Britain there are Hay, Sedbergh and Wigtown; in Europe, Bredevoort in the Netherlands, Tvedestrand and Fjærland in Norway, Sysmä in Finland, Montereggio in Italy, Redu in Belgium, Wünsdorf-Waldstadt in Germany, Urueña in Spain and St-Pierre-de-Clages in Switzerland. Somewhat out on limb, but shoulder to shoulder in spirit with Timbuktu, is Kampung Buku (literally 'Book Village') in Malaysia, situated in a green forest in at the foot of Mt Gunung Raya.

There has been much speculation as to why the book-town concept has worked. A booktown, it has been said, can fare better in terms of civic order than a town that has chosen to base its economy on the ebb and flow of other commodities. A city that thrives on gambling will inevitably see a rise in robbery, drugs, prostitution and fraud. These things are not the stuff of Hay—beyond a one-off and very half-hearted proposal that there be an S&M parlour called The Chain Library. Similarly, a city that relies on the production of cars will fare badly if the cost of production rises and demand falls. Books are not governed by the rules of big business. Furthermore, they have what most people see as an immutable value, totally outstripping their cost of production. A book might be considerably bulkier than a microchip, which can store the text of some 10,000 books, but it has one vital thing in common with it: it is a repository of knowledge, and knowledge confers power, contentment, respectability, in-tellectual stimulation—all these and many other bulwarks against the new barbarism. It is for this reason that Bill Gates and others rescue codices and incunabula and why the ordinary consumer is content to fill his house with books old and new. Books are tangible, beautiful, tactile symbols of our status in the world and of our aspirations. They will last.

A WALK AROUND HAY

This route follows the Wye Valley Walk from Old Black Lion Green (*map p. 159, D2*) as far as the end of Wyeford Road, where a left turn heads along the banks of the Wye, finishing at The Warren.

Old Black Lion Green, where William Seward was stoned (*see p. 59*), lies at the foot of the small lane to the right of the Old Black Lion pub. **Black Lion Well**, in what looks like a private garden but which has public access, is alleged to have interesting properties and the story has something of the flavour of the Wise and Foolish Virgins about it. The waters are said to give the upper hand to whichever of a bridal pair first drinks of them after the wedding. The story goes that a young groom ran swiftly to the well after the ceremony only to discover that his canny bride had taken the precaution of drawing off

her own bottle of well water the night before. The water is said to be blessed by St Keyne, daughter of the legendary 5th-century Welsh king Brychan Brycheiniog (another well, with identical and much publicised properties, can be seen in St Keyne, Cornwall, where she eventually settled).

Heading northeast, the path runs between Dulas Brook and what used to be the outer edge of the **town walls**. Excavations have revealed evidence of industrial activity here over the centuries: grain pits, kilns, tanning, metalworking. As local historian Robert Soldat has pointed out, this is the area of town

View of the River Wye and its watermeadows at the point near
Wyeford Road. When Wordsworth apostrophised the 'sylvan Wye!
thou wanderer thro' the woods …' in his *Tintern Abbey*, he was
thinking of the stretch of the river near Chepstow, but the
description is as apt for Hay and its environs as well.

where much manufacturing
industry was sited. It lies at
the apex of the angle
formed by Dulas Brook and
the Wye, which is down-
wind and downstream of
Hay: all the noxious
by-products of local
industry were kept as far as
possible from the town. It
is likely that Thomas
Howells, at the height of
his wool business (*see p.
29*), would have had
outlying premises in this
area.

Dulas Brook forms the
boundary between Wales
and England, and at this
point it is possible, by
wading out into the water,
to stand with a foot in each
country. This is a good way
of concentrating one's mind

on the swift changes in mood, landscape and architecture that are to be experienced within a very few miles either side of this little stream. Bredwardine, Clifford and Dorstone are resolutely English; nothing could be more Welsh than the ascent to Capel-y-ffin. The two territories are startlingly close together and yet the transition is very swift.

From here the path soon crosses Newport Street, where there is a **plaque commemorating a Town Well**, now gone, as is all trace of the medieval town gate that once stood here.

At the end of **Wyeford Road** the path bears to the left along the banks of the Wye. Wyeford Road, as its name suggests, was the crossing point of the river before the construction of Hay Bridge. The land along the river bank used to be common ground before the advent of the railway. It was for centuries used for recreation by Hay citizens but the railway line and the station (this was nearby, to the north of Wyeford Road) brought this to an end. Sir Joseph Bailey, the Lord of the Manor of Hay (*see box opposite*), remedied the problem in 1884 by constructing a riverside walk that is now known as the **Bailey Walk**, running safely below the railway tracks as far as The Warren from Hay Bridge. In 1887, to commemorate Queen Victoria's Jubilee, the walk was extended as far as Wyeford Road. As a general rule, though the paths are not always continuous and/or passable, one can take one of two routes along the river. The Bailey Walk, on the river bank, has excellent views. The upper path follows the old railway line and is now used by cyclists. It too provides an excellent walk and it is a good idea to switch between the upper and lower paths from time to time.

The finest point in the Bailey Walk, simple but very effective, is halfway down towards the Warren. Here there are the **remains of an old quay** where the barges from Hereford would tie up. There is a stone trough catching the outpouring **Walk Well** and an enchanting view across the Wye. It is as well to be sure-footed on this walk and to bring appropriate footwear. The well makes the path very slippery.

Sir Joseph Bailey (1840–1906)

Joseph Bailey, sometime Lord of the Manor of Hay, was born into a powerful British iron dynasty. His grandfather Joseph and his great-uncle Crawshay were owners of the family ironworks in Nantyglo, South Wales. Both were made of stern and unforgiving stuff. Crawshay was so hated by his workers—they lived and worked in conditions as harsh as his mansion was luxurious—that he was forced to build himself two fortified towers, the Nantyglo Roundhouses. At one point in 1822, during a union insurrection, he was forced to take refuge in one of the towers, protected by a detachment of the Scots Greys. Joseph Bailey Senior, though an austere man, nevertheless put the family fortunes to good use at Hay, constructing the Butter Market (*see p. 50*). His grandson Joseph, by contrast, was a generous spirit. He was, in many ways, a classic product of the Industrial Revolution: a generous benefactor, a Conservative MP (for Hereford) and later Lord Lieutenant of Brecknockshire. He was created Baron Glanusk in 1899. During his career in politics he spent much time at Hay and donated, amongst other things, the Bailey Walk.

Further along the upper path to the left, notice a prominent stone bench. This marks the point to which one can return, after visiting The Warren, and turn off alongside the Login Brook, emerging at St Mary's Church and the motte.

The Warren is an open riverside meadow of considerable beauty that has for centuries been a place for local recreation. The name, it is said, derives from the practice of breeding rabbits here, for consumption by the Lord of the Manor. It seems more likely that there were at any given time sufficient wild rabbits here to ensure a plentiful supply for the castle kitchens. Whatever the position with the rabbits in medieval times, there was certainly a *Watership Down* moment in the early 1970s when proposals were put forward to build a campsite on The Warren. The plan was soon thwarted by a group of local businessmen who clubbed together and bought the site, saving it—and very likely much of the area surrounding it—from certain ruin. The Warren is now in the hands of the Hay Warren Trustees who have, over the years, restored important sites in Hay including the Butter Market.

The Wye embraces The Warren in a slow curve on which, at intervals, there are flights of sparkling rapids. These change position according to the time of year and the strength of the current. There is a unique pebble 'beach' on the bank where the river curves, effectively a lido in the Italian sense, appropriate enough in a town that has an annual arts festival. The views of the tower of St Mary's Church from the river bank are incomparable shortly after sunrise.

ENVIRONS OF HAY

The 18th-century topographer Henry Skyrne visited Hay on his way home to Somerset after a visit to Scotland. He took a guided tour of the surrounding country and tells us he was 'conducted in the course of my rides to several points of view that confirmed me that we need not have gone to Scotland in search of the most striking beauties with which nature has endowed a country'.

CUSOP

Cusop is a Victorian village a short way out of Hay (*map p. 157, C1*). It is reached by heading out on the Bredwardine road and turning right along Dulas Brook, which marks the border between England and Wales. The extravagant Victorian houses lining the way have earned this stretch the local nickname 'Millionaire's Row'. Beyond Cusop itself lies Cusop Dingle. The last recorded sightings of fairies were here; and in conservation circles it is distinguished for having its own proprietary snail, a species of Vitrina unrecorded until its discovery in 1922 by Dr A.E. Boycott of the Royal Society: 'The shell seemed rather flat, the animal was very dark-coloured, and it crawled about with unusual vivacity…'. These characteristics caused the professor to examine the gastropod more closely, only to realise that he had chanced on something new to British fauna. The Dulas Brook is home to otters, kingfishers and trout. But these are small fry compared to the fairies. As the present Vicar of Hay judiciously says, 'If fairies existed, this is where they would most likely be…'. The distinguished folklorist Ella Mary

Leather, in *The Folklore of Herefordshire* (1912), recorded that old people in the village had remembered seeing the fairies dance under the foxgloves in Cusop Dingle. She also refers to the 'Brownie', a mischievous figure much talked about in the households of Cusop and Craswall, who used to sit on the 'sway', the bar holding the ratchet-hook and pot over an open fire. Edging into darker realms, she describes the Old Lady of the Black Mountains, who usually took the form of a poor old woman who would lead a traveller astray on remote roads. This figure is also recorded, sometimes in quite terrifying manifestations, in the Rev. Edmund Jones's *A Relation of Apparitions of Spirits in the County of Monmouth and the Principality of Wales* (1767): 'Of late years there is but little talk about her, the light of the Gospel has driven her to closer quarters—in the coal-pits and holes of the earth, until the day when she shall be gathered in the body to receive the everlasting curse, Math. 25:41. "Depart from me, ye cursed, into everlasting fire, prepared for the devil and his angels".' But the legend persists, despite Jones's reassurance. There is a particularly interesting recent account of a hiker on Hay Bluff who was unfamiliar with the Old Lady legend but had completed some modest research into the apparition of the Virgin at Llanthony. Seeing in the middle distance the figure of a woman dressed in a long cloak with her back to him, he assumed that his research had got the better of his senses. As he drew closer the figure began to turn and he assumed that he would see the Virgin face to face. What he did see, when it turned, he cannot accurately describe and will never forget. Since the expedition, he has never slept more than fitfully at night for an hour or two at most.

Cusop is the burial place of the wretched William Seward (*see p. 59*). A plaque in the church commemorates him.

View from Cusop churchyard.

LLANIGON

A good starting point for an exploration of the surrounding area is the village of Llanigon, two miles southwest of Hay (*map p. 156, B2*). It is a small place today, but in early Norman times it was the mother parish of Hay; the two were separated by William Revel in the early 12th century. It has other claims to fame: the hymn writer William Williams Pantycelyn was educated at a dissenters' academy here; and Francis Kilvert fell in love with the parson's daughter, whose father forbade the union on the grounds that Kilvert was insufficiently provided for.

The main building of interest in the village is the **church of St Eigon**, set in an ancient circular churchyard. There is some debate about the dedication, purists opting for the male St Eigon, Bishop and Confessor, and those of a more

View of Lord Hereford's Knob from Gospel Pass, the defile that leads through two spurs of the Black Mountains into the Vale of Ewyas.

romantic inclincation favouring St Eigon, or Eurgain, daughter of Caractus and foundress of a 6th-century college of Christian Druids. Though the building bears traces of Norman work, it is predominantly of the 15th–17th centuries. The upper storey of the 14th-century porch was once the living quarters of the priest, a situation eloquent of past austerity in this part of the world: what must his quarters have been like in midwinter? There are now three bells in this upper storey, all dated 1670, the date at which the priest's lodging was transformed into a bell-stage. Note the unusual half-round mouldings that support it. In the porch there is a 13th-century or earlier font, with three lines incised in the rim. The church interior was restored in 1857 and there are handsome numbered and gated pews.

During the restoration the 18th-century two-decker pulpit was divided, one half becoming the priest's stall.

Into the Black Mountains

From Llanigon drive south towards Abergavenny, taking the single-track mountain route and ensuring that you set off in reasonable weather. A slight, apparently harmless snowfall in Hay or Llanigon is an almost certain sign of blizzard conditions further up in the Vale of Ewyas. In any case, the colossal beauties of the hills are best seen in crystal clear light. It is worth pulling up halfway towards Capel-y-ffin and contemplating the **views towards Hay Bluff and Lord Hereford's Knob**. They have a stunning supernatural beauty, perhaps because the normal principles of linear and aerial perspective seem not to apply, a failing that dismayed 18th-century travellers, who liked to see Nature brought to heel, but which is a revelation to modern eyes.

The **Offa's Dyke Path** runs along the ridge of the eastern spur of the Black Mountains here. Walkers can park their car by the stone circle at the foot of Hay Bluff and from there walk to Llanthony or to Capel-y-ffin. Those familiar with Chatwin's *On the Black Hill* will recognise some place names (Red Daren; The Vision Farm; Cockalofty).

Bruce Chatwin (1940–89)
Chatwin was the author of *On the Black Hill*, a novel set on the border of Herefordshire in England and Radnorshire in Wales. This novel, which won the James Tait Black Memorial Prize when it was published in 1982, recreated the harsh tenor of rural life at the beginning of the 20th ➤

century and its spiritually paralysing effect on the central characters, Lewis and Benjamin Jones. The twin brothers live on a farm, The Vision, with their parents Amos and Mary and their sister Rebecca. We learn early on that the national border runs through the farmhouse itself: 'One of the windows looked out over the green fields of England: the other looked back into Wales…'. The remorseless dysfunctionality of the Jones family is played out against the imperious majesty of the landscape and the ingrained malice of the small local community. A defining moment, recounted with humour blacker than the hill, is when Amos, the head of the family, wounds his wife in the eye with the book she is reading, enraged by her enjoyment of something that is inaccessible to him because of his limited education.

Chatwin was a brilliant but restless spirit who came late to writing after an early career as an art expert and, briefly, an archaeologist. The story that sums up his approach to life begins when he was sent by the *Sunday Times Magazine* to interview the 93-year-old architect and designer Eileen Gray in Paris. In her apartment, he caught sight of a map she had painted of the area of South America called Patagonia. 'I've always wanted to go there,' he told her. 'So have I,' she replied, 'go there for me.' He did, and the resulting book, *In Patagonia*, established him as a travel writer and formed the foundation of his literary career. He was one of the first prominent men in England to contract HIV, a setback he greeted with a unique species of uplifting and imaginative denial. There was no question for Chatwin of any mealy-mouthed coming out. When anxious friends tackled him about his increasingly intrusive symptoms he brushed them off. It was a fungal infection; he had been unexpectedly bitten by a Chinese bat. When the truth inevitably came out he invented a number of stories about how he had contracted the virus. He had been gang-raped in Dahomey; Robert Mapplethorpe's lover had infected him; and so on. When the game was up he summoned his friend Werner Herzog and gave him his prized leather rucksack saying 'You're the one who has to wear it now, you're the one who's walking'.

CAPEL-Y-FFIN

Capel-y-ffin (*map p. 157, C3*) is known for its natural beauty, for its religious associations, and for having once been the home of Eric Gill. All three of these things can still be appreciated here, the first more particularly if you arrive on foot.

St Mary's

St Mary's Church, Capel-y-ffin, is a chapel of ease to Llanigon. It is one of the smallest in the country, only 8m by 4m inside. Though tiny, it is certainly one of the most beautiful places of worship of any faith to be found anywhere. Francis Kilvert thought nothing of walking the nine miles here from Clyro and loved the 'old chapel, short, stout and boxy, with its little bell turret, squatting like a stout grey owl among its seven great yews'. The charmingly lopsided belfry has two bells, one medieval but recast in the 19th century. In the churchyard there is a small, compact, powerful **headstone by Eric Gill**. Etched into the plain glass arched window above the altar is an appropriate text from Psalm 121: 'I will lift up mine eyes unto the hills, from whence cometh my help'. The church was built in 1762 replacing an earlier chapel, and the south porch was added in 1817. The small oblong interior has a gallery along the west and south walls ensuring that all of the seating faces the pulpit, which is octagonal, built of timber, and dated 1780. There is an early medieval font.

Nearby, accessible by a stile, is the **Moravian Baptist Chapel** that doubled as school in the 19th century. The churchyard contains some fine headstones. Note the rust-coloured decay on a group of them, traditionally said to be the blood of martyrs.

The former Anglican Monastery

Turn right about 50 yards south of the churchyard and head for the site of the **former Anglican Monastery and Church of Llanthony Tertia,** founded in 1870 by the eccentric Anglican lay reader Joseph Leycester Lyne, who took the religious name of Father Ignatius. Lyne, a controversial figure to this day, was so inspired by the monastic revival of the late 19th century that he set out to found a new Anglican order. He was unable to persuade any of the Anglican bishops to ordain him, but he did not let this deter him from his objective. He managed to buy land in Wales and settle in with a group of professed monks and novices. Llanthony Tertia is so called because Father Ignatius intended it as the successor of Llanthony Prima (*see overleaf*) and Llanthony Secunda in Gloucester, the first great priories. Opinions vary as to Lyne's integrity; Kilvert described him as 'a gentle man of simple manners… entirely possessed by his one ideal'. His finest hour came

The tiny church of St Mary, Capel-y-ffin.

unexpectedly and did little to boost his standing in Anglican circles: 'There were some boys who received their education in the Abbey. They were playing in the fields one summer evening, but abandoned their game and ran to Father Ignatius, crying out that there was a light burning in a bush. He calmed them, and ordered a watch to be kept before the altar by the monks of the Abbey and the nuns in the Convent near by…. The next day one of the nuns sent word that Father Ignatius had left the monstrance on the altar… Father Ignatius went to lock it up, but it was not visible… On that evening the boys saw the light in the bush again. The monks were assembled in the porch, where they sang an Ave…. It was a foul night. The wind howled in the vast solitude. The rain teemed down. A thick pall of cloud draped the hills and the heavens. A wonderful light appeared in the heavens. It seemed to open out, and in the centre there then appeared the Blessed Virgin Mary. Her hands were outstretched, and the light from her presence was so radiant that the monks could hardly look upon it. The walls of the massive monastery became like glass.' (Testimony of one of Fr. Ignatius's monks—who, interestingly, renounced his vows to become a bus conductor—quoted in *Lead, Kindly Light: Studies of Saints and Heroes of the Oxford Movement* by Desmond Morse-Boycott.) From that point onward, pilgrims steadily beat a path to the door. Today, the trustees plan to renovate the ruined church as a focal point for the considerable following that Father Ignatius still has. The domestic buildings of the monastery are privately owned and cannot be viewed but it is interesting to note that within their walls is Capel-y-ffin's third—Roman Catholic—chapel.

In 1924, after Lyne's death, Llanthony Tertia became the **home of the sculptor Eric Gill**. His granddaughter, Mary Griffiths, lives nearby at The Grange, which she and her daughter run as a B&B. Their charming house, known romantically as the House of Guinevere, is a good base from which to explore the local countryside on foot or on horseback. Eric Gill, like Father Ignatius, was a peculiar character whom it is easy to malign. The intensity of his religious belief and his dedication to his art is for many hard to reconcile with the unsettling details of his sexual life that he revealed in his journals and celebrated in his powerful erotic drawings. As is witnessed by the headstone at Capel-y-ffin, he brought high art to monumental masonry. His typefaces, Gill Sans, Perpetua and others, are classics. The BBC chose Gills Sans as the font for its wordmark. Blue Guides also use the font for all its headers and captions.

Eric Gill: *The Bath* (1920).

LLANTHONY PRIORY

Llanthony Priory (Llanthony Prima; *map p. 157, D3*), one of the earliest houses of Augustinian canons founded in Britain, lies in ruins high up in the Vale of Ewyas. It is said

that William de Lacy chose the spot while out hunting, having taken cover in a small hillside chapel dedicated to St David. A church soon followed, and by 1130 there were 40 canons in residence. The historian Gerald of Wales described the site as being 'fixt among barbarous people', and this turned out to be a fair comment. By 1135 the local inhabitants had forced the newcomers to beat a retreat to Hereford and Gloucester, in which latter city a daughter foundation, Llanthony Secunda, was set up. The de Lacy family persisted in the area—the retreat to Gloucester was never regarded as anything more than temporary setback —and by the middle of the 13th century they had recreated, on the ruins of the first priory, a vast medieval masterpiece. Even in ruin, the scale is impressive, an extravaganza of transitional Norman–Gothic that is clearly the result of a collaboration between rich patrons and sophisticated builders.

After the rebellion of Owain Glyndwr and the Dissolution of the Monasteries, Llanthony fell slowly into decay. Its new life as a tourist attraction began in earnest in the 18th century. In 1803 the artist and dilletante Sir Richard Colt-Hoare witnessed at first hand the collapse of the great west window. As one would expect, Llanthony has been well recorded by artists. The ruin played an important part in J.M.W. Turner's early development, his transition from comparatively formal representations of landscape to the full-blown romantic celebrations for which he is best known. An early watercolour from c. 1792 (now in Indianapolis State Museum) depicts a rainswept Llanthony

The ruins of the 12th-century Llanthony Priory, set in the beautiful Vale of Ewyas, the valley of the Honddu river.

View of Llanthony by J.M.W. Turner (c. 1792), painted before the collapse of the west window, in an early, pre-Impressionistic style.

with dash and confidence. A later work, also in Indianapolis, is much more Impressionistic.

In the 19th century Llanthony Priory was acquired by the poet Walter Savage Landor, who had the intention of setting up as a model local squire despite glaring historical evidence that over-imperious newcomers are not accorded the warmest of welcomes in this locale. He soon left, his attempts to improve the peasantry frustrated by unreliable tenants and a parasitical local solicitor. But before the dream turned sour, he relished life here, describing nightingales and glow-worms in the valley to his friend Robert Southey. He refused to sell the Priory to Father Ignatius.

CLYRO

A little over a mile to the south of Hay is the village of Clyro (meaning 'clear water'; *map p. 156, B1*), best known as the parish where Francis Kilvert was curate, from 1863–64. His old church, the **parish church of St Michael**, was rebuilt by Thomas Nicholson in 1853. The tower is old, Late Perpendicular up as far as the clock stage, but raised (in 1894) after that. The churchyard is pleasant and contains many interesting monuments. These include a late 18th-century memorial to Herbert Beaven and one of 1830 to Elizabeth Williams.

Kilvert's erstwhile home, Ashbrook House, is now an art gallery, **The Kilvert Gallery**. The house has a fine Regency staircase window. Kilvert enthusiasts will remember that the history teacher A.L. Le Quesne lived here for over a year and immersed himself in Kilvert's life, taking the same walks and keeping a daily journal of his own experiences and insights. The resulting book, *After Kilvert*, remains a valuable and unusual literary classic and gives great insight not only into the Curate of Clyro's life and work but also into the society of the time.

Just outside the village is Clyro Court, now the **Baskerville Hall Hotel**, a florid 19th-century Jacobean-style mansion built for Sir Thomas Mynors Baskerville, a friend of Sir Arthur Conan-Doyle, who was a frequent guest here. When writing *The Hound of the Baskervilles*, Conan-Doyle was inspired by various eerie locations in Britain but it is clear that he borrowed his friend's name for the story. Thomas Baskerville was said to be happy with this on the condition that Conan-Doyle set the story elsewhere so as to avoid an influx of inquisitive tourists.

Whereas there is no sign of Roman settlement at Hay, there are the remains of a substantial **vexillation fortress** here (very close to Boatside Farm; *map p. 157, C1; see illustration on p. 14*) and a marching camp. We know from Tacitus (*Annals XII, xxxviii*) that the local tribe, the Silures, were a nuisance to the Romans and a formidable enemy: 'A camp-prefect and some legionary cohorts, left behind to construct garrison-posts in Silurian territory, were attacked from all quarters; and, if relief had not quickly reached the invested troops from the neighbouring forts—they had been informed by messenger—they must have perished to the last man. As it was, the prefect fell, with eight centurions and the boldest members of the rank and file.'

Francis Kilvert (1840–79)
The Curate of Clyro's Diaries are well known and greatly loved. 'He being dead, yet speaketh' is the apt inscription on his grave at Bredwardine. Kilvert's affection for the countryside and its people make moving reading: 'Good Friday, 15 April 1870. The walk across the fields in the glowing hot sunshine, the country basked lovely and peaceful. I saw one man ploughing on Ty-yr-mynach and met no one else till I came to Hay Bridge where the long empty sunny white road stretched away straight over the river to the town, the picturesque little border town with its slate-roofed houses climbing and shining up the hill crested by the dark long mass of the old ivy-grown castle with its huge war-broken tower'. He is certainly one of the great English diarists and his writing has been compared with that of Proust, Pepys, Amiel, Gerard Manley Hopkins and

D.H. Lawrence. Yet we would know nothing at all of this talent had it not been for the publisher's reader at Jonathan Cape who discovered him: William Plomer. In Chapter 13 of his memoirs, *At Home*, Plomer recounts this wonderful discovery, setting the scene by telling us what a reader might reasonably expect to find on his desk on any given morning: 'experimental verse by some boy or girl', 'a charwoman's memoirs, or some crazy dotard's demonstration, by means of numerology or cryptograms, that Bacon was the Dark Lady of the Sonnets', or 'the diary of a carriage tour kept by a young lady who visited the field of Waterloo'. In the light of all this, he explains, to receive a couple of old notebooks from a man in Dorset 'was not in itself therefore to feel pressure on the trigger of expectation'. But when Plomer opened the notebooks, he saw all the splendour of the Black Mountains revealed, all the passionate inner life of the diarist laid bare, all the idiosyncrasies and customs of his flock described with love, humour and eloquence. Plomer, as editor of Kilvert's diaries in the '50s, was in the enviable position of being able to meet people who had known and who remembered him. They give a clear picture of how popular he was as man and priest. A Mrs Amey from Cusop recalled how, when Kilvert returned from his honeymoon, local men took the two black horses out of the shafts of his carriage and pulled it back to the vicarage themselves through the pouring rain. It was a cruel turn of fortune that when he finally fell in love, and married Elizabeth Ann Rowland, the happiness was short-lived. Kilvert died of peritonitis only a few days after returning from their honeymoon in Scotland.➤

He seemed genuinely to have had what he himself called a 'strange and terrible gift of exciting love' and a cousin described him as 'very sleek and glossy and gentle, rather like a nice Newfoundland dog'. It is easy to bring to mind, when walking further afield in Kilvert's footsteps amid the colossal beauties of the Vale of Ewyas, V.S. Pritchett's words: 'When we contrast the note and rhythm of our lives with those of Kilvert's, we see there is more than a change of fashion between the generations. We perceive with shock that it is we who are unnatural, because we do not live within the walls of a long period of civilization and peace'. But it would be a mistake to think that Kilvert's arcadia is merely a pleasing literary relic of a long-gone rural past. His great compassion, his high good humour, the uninhibited freshness with which he engages with beauty—all these mark him out as a man for all time, forever striding purposefully and jubilantly across the fields to Hay.

BREDWARDINE, DORSTONE & PETERCHURCH

Bredwardine

Francis Kilvert was made Vicar of Bredwardine in 1877, and retained the position until his early death two years later. He is buried in the churchyard, his **memorial** bearing a singularly appropriate inscription (*see p. 110*). Also in the churchyard are the remains of a fine medieval **preaching cross**. The church, dedicated to St Andrew, contains two

The enigmatic carvings over the north door of Bredwardine church, variously interpreted as Egyptian gods and the Virgin and Child.

interesting memorials. The huge recumbent man in 14th-century armour, the '**Bredwardine Giant**', is said to be Walter Baskerville (d. 1369). The **alabaster tomb** to the right of the altar is that of Sir Ralph Baskerville, who was killed at Agincourt. There is a massive font, possibly 12th-century, mounted on disproportionately delicate columns. The lower section of the north wall shows possibly late Saxon or early Norman herringbone masonry. The south doorway has a worn Romanesque tympanum and attractive capitals. Of considerable interest are the two sandstone **figures carved over the north door**, the left-hand figure a strange amalgam of bird and serpent and the right a grotesque ape-like creature. There has inevitably been much speculation as to what they might signify. The Rev. Greville Chester (1890) saw the Egyptian dwarf-god Bes and the falcon-headed moon-god Khons. G. Marshall (1918) saw 'a basilisk and Christ in Majesty'. E. Gethyn-Jones (1979) compared the figures to the capitals at Lavardin (Loir-et-Cher) representing St Benedict and the Virgin and Child. It is of interest that there are similar figures nearby at Letton and Willersley. It is possible that the right-hand figure is a sheela-na-gig, an ancient fertility symbol.

From St Andrew's Church there are footpaths to the Wye in one direction and to the **ruins of Bredwardine Castle** in the other.

Dorstone

Due south of Bredwardine and only four miles from Hay is the village of Dorstone (*map p. 157, D1*). Between the two is the clearly signposted **Arthur's Stone**. In common with many early remains of this sort in Britain, it has been endowed over the ages with an entertaining but spurious Arthurian association. It is, in reality, a Neolithic chamber tomb dating from 3700 BC–2700 BC, and is a very fine example. The massive and striking fallen slabs that mark

The megalithic chamber tomb known as Arthur's Stone at Dorstone (4th–3rd millennium BC).

the site are situated on the ridge line of a hill overlooking both the Golden Valley and the Wye Valley.

Dorstone's other claim to attention is a **stone found in its church** inscribed with the words *Hanc capellam ex voto ad Mariam Virginam, Richardus de Brito dedicavit* (This Chapel is dedicated to the Virgin Mary, in fulfilment of a vow, by Richard de Brito, 1256), reinforcing the story that de Brito, one of the knights who assassinated Thomas Becket, built this church in a bid for expiation. One of the church bells bears an inscription in Latin promising that it will ring for eternity. The rare pewter Dorstone Chalice was stolen in 2005. The vicar would very much like to have it back if any collectors or dealers chance on it.

Peterchurch

Peterchurch lies southeast of Dorstone (*map p. 157, D2*). There is good **walking country** around here, in the Golden Valley and along the Herefordshire Trail. Everything is fertile and tranquilly lovely; it is very different from the sublime escarpments of the Black Mountains just across the border.

Peterchurch **church spire** is made of fibreglass—a cost-effective solution that is not as rare as one might imagine. The church interior contains a locally well-known plaster panel depicting the **Peterchurch Trout**, reputed to have been caught in a nearby pool with a golden chain about its neck. This story gradually became associated, in terms of Christian symbolism, with a legend that St Peter passed through this area and blessed a spring. A quaint local custom is recorded by Compton Reade in *Memorials of Old Herefordshire* (1904): 'At Peterchurch there is a piece of land called the "Dog Acre". It was bequeathed to Peterchurch

Evelyn de Morgan: *Queen Eleanor and Fair Rosamund* (c. 1905).

to be held by the "dog-whipper", whose duty it was to drive stray dogs from the church. A man named Perks held this office within comparatively recent times, and he had one of the special implements, "something like wooden tongs", which were used for the purpose.'

CLIFFORD & WHITNEY-ON-WYE

Clifford (*map p. 157, C1*) contains a number of points of interest, including the remains of a substantial **Roman fortress**. The ruins of the imposing **Clifford Castle** (*no access but ruins visible*) are nearby overlooking the Wye. Many of the houses in the village are clearly constructed from material plundered from it: close inspection reveals massive blocks in tiny houses, in a make-do-and-mend approach to building that was once the norm near historical sites like this. Clifford is perhaps best known as the family home of Sir Walter de Clifford's daughter, 'Fair Rosamund', who was said to be one of the most beautiful women in the world and was the mistress of Henry II. She has been a great source of inspiration for generations of poets and painters and there are many stories about her of the *si non è vero, è ben trovato* persuasion. Of these, the most appealing are that Henry kept her in a hunting lodge in the middle of a maze in Woodstock and that she was imaginatively killed, by being roasted alive, by Henry's jealous wife Eleanor of Aquitaine. There is an extremely unsettling painting by Evelyn de Morgan showing Eleanor confronting Rosamund in the secret bower, in which the queen is depicted in full Cruella de Ville mode (*illustrated opposite*). She carries a cup of some bright red deadly liquor, the poison which in other versions of the tale she forced Fair Rosamund to drink. In her other hand she carries the string that has led her to the lover's trysting place. Rosamund was buried in Godstow nunnery near Oxford with, it is said, the following epitaph upon her tomb: *Hic jacet in tomba Rosa Mundi, non Rosa Munda, Non redolet, sed olet, quæ redolere solet* (Here lies entombed the Rose of the World, not a pure rose: she smelleth not sweet but stinketh, that was wont to have such fragrance).

In the parish **church of St Mary** (of ancient foundation but substantially restored in the 19th century), in a recess on the north side of the chancel, is a large and very fine carved oak effigy of a priest in Eucharistic garments, one of only a few hundred such medieval effigies in Britain and in excellent condition. For comparison, the only other such effigy in Herefordshire is at Much Marcle, near Ross-on-Wye. Unlike the Clifford effigy, it bears traces of the original paintwork, which would have been strikingly colourful.

Whitney-on-Wye

Whitney-on-Wye (*map p. 157, C1*) lies on the Hereford Road. There are good **views of the Wye** and the toll bridge from the Boat Inn. The **church** was built in 1740 to replace an earlier church on the north bank that was swept away in the floods of 1735. The sanctuary reredos is made of 17th-century oak from Whitney Court; a centre panel bears the date 1624. The communion rails are from 1740. Rest and refreshment are afforded by the **Rhydspence**, an old drover's inn nearby to the west.

Interior of the old Rhydspence Inn, a 14th-century manor-turned-drovers'-hostelry.

MAESYRONNEN CHAPEL

Maesyronnen (*map p. 156, B1*; pron: *Mice-uh-ronnen*) is the oldest, most venerable Nonconformist place of worship in Wales. The chapel dates from 1697 and was converted from a cruck-framed barn that may well date back to the 15th century, an innovation not unusual at a time when Nonconformists would gladly adapt domestic buildings for worship. Prior to the Act of Toleration in 1689, it may well have been the case that Maesyronnen and similarly remote sites were used as secret meeting places. The decision to convert the barn is likely to have been founded on a history of covert worship or meeting on the site. Maesyronnen is associated, for example, with the Welsh Nonconformist Puritan preacher Vavasour Powell who preached in Wales as early as 1640. Henry Maurice, the leading Nonconformist preacher and minister at Llanigon, used the farmhouse for meetings from the early 1670s. The chapel conveys a vivid sense of the adventurous simplicity of Nonconformism in the early days. The church furniture, simple box pews and a high pulpit, were added as and when funds from the congregation permitted: a pew and a table, for example, are later additions and dated 1727. The walls are completely plain save for an exhortation to 'Praise God in His Sanctuary' (Psalm 150) and a number of simple but moving memorial tablets, many of which reflect the low life expectancy prevalent at the beginning of 19th century. Ten memorials record the deaths of three children in infancy and of seven other young persons aged 7, 13, 19, 21, 27, 28 and 29. Cromwell is said to have visited. The adjacent cottage was added c. 1750 and can be rented from the Landmark Trust for short holiday lets (*see p. 132*).

PRACTICAL INFORMATION

FOOD & DRINK IN HAY

It was said only a few years ago that there is little to do in Hay apart from becoming a drunk or a religious maniac. Nowadays, since the town is richly furnished by places of worship and bars, it is possible to become either or both without too much application. In 1922 the *Gloucester Chronicle* published a series of damning reports compiled in the previous century entitled 'Morals in Brecknockshire', 'Morals in Cardiganshire', 'Morals in Radnorshire' and so on. Local clergy, magistrates, shopkeepers and working men were asked to comment on the moral health of their county. Few were able to give a favourable diagnosis. The Vicar of Hay, William Latham Bevan, commented that 'Drunkenness and illegitimacy are the prevailing vices of the neighbourhood. Very many of the poorer classes are ruined by this indulgence in the first, while the second is considered as a very venial offence. A promise of marriage on the part of the man seems to legitimatise the whole affair in the eyes of the parties themselves as well as in the estimation of their friends'.

Despite the best efforts of Bevan, the teetotallers never gained as strong a foothold in the neighbourhood as the Hay Foresters, a society that counselled moderation. Nevertheless, occasional meetings were held here by the Rechabites, the leading teetotal Friendly Society, founded on a verse from the Book of Jeremiah (35:5–6) which tells how the sons of Rechab, when tempted by pots of wine, refused it. (Rechab the Kenite, it should be noted, is increasingly misreferred to as 'Rehab' these days.)

Sign in Clyro.

At all events, the strictures and controversies of the past are now mere diversions. Locals, if pressed, may well complain that there are few places to go of an evening but visitors will soon notice that there is a great deal to do in Hay, all year round. Some pubs and restaurants occupy buildings of architectural merit—one does not often come across a Grade II listed fish and chip shop. All pubs and restaurants mentioned here vary enormously in terms of food and atmosphere and most visitors will manage to find something that suits their taste.

Pubs and bars

The Wheatsheaf: Many years ago it would not have been unusual to find April Ashley seated at the bar here, a picture of elegance with immaculately painted toenails and accompanied by her diamanté-collared whippet, holding forth on love and life in Hay and Hampstead and all points between. Nowadays this is more of a place to relax over a few cheerful pints with the younger set in Hay, chewing over local gossip and heatedly discussing the latest sports results. *38 Lion St; map p. 159, C2.*

The Three Tuns: This is one of the oldest and architecturally most venerable buildings in Hay, a 16th-century hall sporting cruck-truss beams with evidence of later 17th-century expansion. This pub was a noted centre of Bohemian life under the aegis of its former owner, the legendary Lucy Powell, who was accorded the status of a living saint at the court of King Richard. It remains a magnet for celebrities, but these days, since Lucy died and the pub was sold on, it is more of a restaurant than a Bohemian meeting place. It serves good-quality gourmet food and the interior opens out, following damage and restoration some five years ago, into a huge, well-heated space with a number of the 16th- and 17th-century features exposed wherever possible. The huge chimney rises the full height of the building, with fireplaces on both floors. *Broad St, T: 01497 821855, www.three-tuns.com; map p. 159, C1.*

Kilvert's Hotel: Despite the name, this place has no historical connection with Kilvert, though one senses the Curate of Clyro would probably approve of the good-natured banter that takes place on any given night between locals and visitors. Dogs are welcome, and there is quite often a semi-recumbent pile of them in varying states of repose or wariness, either at the bar or by the wood-burning stove. The roast lunches are vast and excellent. The open square in front of Kilvert's is known as the Bullring, because livestock was traded here in the 19th century. *Bullring, T: 01497 821042; map p. 159, C2.*

The Rose and Crown: A quiet pub with attractively low ceilings and a warm atmosphere. *Broad St, T: 01497 820435; map p. 158, B2.*

The Blue Boar: Kilvert recalls graphically the time when Wombwell's Menagerie visited Hay and the stables of the Blue Boar were filled to bursting point with exotic animals, including camels and bears. There are two open fireplaces and three dining spaces clustered around the bar. The food is good, especially the *boeuf bourgignon* and the Beef Wellington. The venison is striking—a Woodstock of the palate. American visitors may note that from the First World War onwards there were dances held at the Drill Hall on Lion St. These were enthusiastically attended by American servicemen in the Second World War, who predictably came in for a good deal of flak from the locals, flabbergasted by the comparative informality prevailing in the US ranks. It was not uncommon, when a detachment of infantrymen was marching through the town, for a couple of thirsty stragglers to break away and grab a quick half pint from the

Blue Boar. *Castle St, T: 01497 820884; map p. 158, B3.*

The Famous Old Black Lion Inn: 'Just how an old inn should be', according to the *Daily Telegraph*. The 17th-century premises, with later Georgian additions, are warm and attractively decorated, a good staging-post for those starting or finishing Hay's stretch of the Wye Valley Walk which starts at Black Lion Green. Rory Bremner has dined here, as have Jimmy Carter, Edward Woodward and Ian Botham. A local wit is fond of saying that Mr Bremner merely impersonated these last three, effecting quick changes between courses. *Lion St, T: 01497 820841, www.oldblacklion.co.uk; map p. 159, D2.*

The Swan at Hay: Large, elegant Grade II listed Georgian coaching inn with a number of facilities including a public bar, an informal bistro and, overlooking the walled garden, an elegant restaurant with a striking carved fireplace. It is run by the Mackintosh family who also own the Bull's Head at Craswall (*see p. 130*). *Church St, T: 01497 821188, www.swanathay.co.uk; map p. 158, A3.*

The Royal British Legion: Decidedly not a hotbed of radicalism nor an ideal venue for a quiet, meditative drink. It is a lively private club that extends a warm welcome to visitors— ask to be signed in—and offers a good selection of the local ales. The Legion participates actively in the life of Hay, organising year-round outings and events, including gliding at the Black Mountains Gliding Club and, in June, Ladies Day at Hereford Racecourse. *Market St, T: 01497 821754; map p. 159, C2.*

Restaurants

The Granary: Pleasant two-storey restaurant housed in an early 19th-century wool store. Good vegetarian and vegan options. The upper room has changing exhibitions by contemporary artists and there is a permanent display of local advertising material relating to past businesses in Hay. Free WiFi. *Broad St, T: 01497 820790; map p. 158, B2.*

Oscars Bistro: Popular with locals, offering straightforward, well-made food. *High Town, T: 01497 821193; map p. 159, C2.*

Red Indigo: This is Hay's deservedly successful curry house, decorated in high Bollywood chic to the extent that it would be easy to imagine actresses like Raveena Tandon or Karisma Kapoor sashaying through the elegant rooms. Red Indigo possesses, unusually for an Indian restaurant, a small garden overlooking the Wye Valley. The combination of good food, good atmosphere and the great outdoors might easily persuade any would-be Penelope Chetwodes to abandon the long haul to Himachal Pradesh and stick to Hay. *Castle St, corner of Belmont Rd, T: 01497 821999; map p. 158, B2.*

Chop Suey House: A cheerful, high-standard Chinese takeaway next to Richard Booth's Bookshop. *Lion St; map p. 159, C2.*

Cafés and tearooms

The Sandwich Cellar on Backfold is popular with walkers putting together a picnic. It is also popular with the local book trade at lunchtime so it is advisable to get your picnic done earlier in the day. Also on Backfold is **Bone China**, a tiny tea room with tables outside in fine weather.

The Chamaeleon & Coffee Shop Isis (*8 Castle St*) is a good stop for all day breakfast, cakes, tea and coffee. There is a gift section selling kites, crystals, cards and carvings.

Shepherds Icecream (*9 High Town*) is favoured by locals as a stop for take-away coffees and by everyone for its ice cream.

The Old Stables Tearoom in Bear St has won an impressive number of awards. Coffee, lunch, tea; there is an open fire.

Café Hay @ The Craft Centre on Oxford St serves breakfast, lunch and tea seven days a week.

Two curiosities

There are two unusual and easily overlooked buildings in Broad Sreet. These are **The Fish and Chip Shop**, housed in a small, late Victorian building of considerable charm, dated 1896. The gabled front in Flemish bond brick is decorated with chevron banding and pleasing daisy ornaments and the slate roof has ridge cresting and wave ornamented barge boards. A tablet bears the initials

'TW', said to be a member of the influential Wellington family of Hay Castle. The chippy's finest hour came in December 1993, when convicted armed robber Edward Mark Williams held a group of residents hostage in what was then the dental surgery in 43 Lion St. The town was descended on by a phalanx of armed police and a detachment of SAS. They and the many film crews who came to cover the event ordered a constant supply of fish and chips all through the night. Eventually, at 5 in the morning, Williams dozed off. One of the woman hostages attacked him with an umbrella while another, the dental hygienist Mrs Davies, got possession of the gun. Williams got four life sentences.

The Open House and Sensory Garden, further along, is an intriguing little building, used for weekly Christian gatherings. It appears to have missed the attention of the listing authority or, at any rate, not to have been officially recorded. The construction is of stone with timber cladding, late Victorian in feel, like a small traditional reading-room. The trustees have created an excellent 'sensory garden' to the rear of the premises, with outdoor seating and tables. This comes into its own in spring and summer, when blind or partially-sighted visitors are able to enjoy the flowers and herbs and a few tactile art installations. The Open House serves tea on Thursdays and it is possible to picnic in the garden at all times.

THE GLOBE GALLERY

The Globe Gallery arts centre in Newport Street (*map p. 159, C1*), is housed in the former Ebenezer United Reform Church, an elegant building completed in 1845 under the supervision of its Methodist minister, the Rev. David Griffiths. The exterior retains all of the original 19th-century features, notably the hipped slate roof and the elegant sash windows. The interior, in pleasing contrast, has been opened out into a versatile performance space with a restaurant and bar, informally dispersed sofas and tables, a gallery and a small stage. Upstairs in a gallery there is another projection area with armchairs, tables and sofas set aside mainly for music videos. The cellar is used for film screenings, meetings and recitals.

Of the old church furnishings, the Gothic timber pulpit has been preserved and is often used in performances, an innovation that may well be smiled on, a little ruefully perhaps, by the shade of its erstwhile occupant, David Griffiths, who later became well known as a missionary in Madagascar and for his translation of the Bible into Malagasy.

There is an impressive range of food served throughout the day; among many inspiring offerings is a good Welsh Rarebit (*see p. 137*). During the day art films are often projected onto the vast wall.

The building is owned by Hilary Lawson, a philosopher, film-maker and video artist, Director of the Institute of Art and Ideas, founder of the Artscape Project and a director of TVF Media. Over the last three years he has tranformed the Globe into a performance and exhibition space, ideal for showcasing all kinds of creative work. Lawson is aiming to provide a venue that will rival the out-of-town Hay Festival site and encourage performers and writers of stature to perform in the town centre itself. The concept is catching on, and other venues in Hay, notably Richard Booth's Bookshop, are making space available for year-round performances, readings and screenings.

WHERE TO EAT AROUND HAY

East of Hay (Herefordshire, England)

The **Bull's Head at Craswall** is an outstanding pub with an excellent restaurant. The owner, chef Harry Mackintosh, trained in France. (*T: 01981 510616, www.thebullsheadcraswall.co.uk; map p. 157, C2*). Also in Craswall is **White Haywood Farm**, which serves home-raised beef, pork and lamb. It also offers B&B accommodation. (*T: 01981 510324, www.blackmountainsfarmrestaurant.co.uk; map p. 157, C2*).

The **Rhydspence Inn** west of Whitney-on-Wye is a 14th-century drovers' inn serving excellent food. (*T: 01497 831262, www.rhydspence-inn.co.uk; map p. 157, C1*).

The **Pandy Inn** at Dorstone is reputed to be the oldest pub in Herefordshire, probably dating from the 12th century. It serves good fresh fish and vegetarian dishes, as well as local lamb, of course (*T: 01981 550277, www.pandyinn. co.uk; map p. 157, D1*).

West of Hay (Powys, Wales)

The **Half Moon Hotel** at Llanthony, Abergavenny makes a good stop for food and ale after what can be an exercising round trip taking in the Priory and Capel-y-ffin (*T: 01873 890611; map p. 157, D3*). At the Priory itself, you can eat either in the restaurant of the **Priory Hotel** or in the snug, low-vaulted bar. No dogs, no children under 10. (*T: 01873 890487, www.llanthonyprioryhotel.co.uk; map p. 157, D3*)

The **Felin Fach Griffin** at Felinfach has been described by AA Gill as 'exceptional anywhere in Europe'. The place has become something of a destination in itself, and has won a flutter of awards. Lovingly run by people who know what they're doing, the food is delicious and unpretentious (much of it from their own kitchen garden) and the wine list superb. (*T: 01874 620111, www.eatdrinksleep.ltd.uk; map p. 156, A2*).

ACCOMMODATION

There are plenty of places to stay in Hay and its environs (and during Festival season, there need to be), running the gamut from fine hotels to campsites. The **Swan at Hay** offers excellent rooms (ask for Room 3), and a fine garden in which to reflect after a long day (*Church St, T: 01497 821188, www.swanathay.co.uk; map p. 158, A3*). The **Famous Old Black Lion** on Lion St (*T: 01497 820841, www.oldblacklion.co.uk; map p. 159, D2*) has ten well-appointed bedrooms. **Tinto House** is an elegant 18th-century town house with a garden overlooking the Wye and nicely furnished, comfortable rooms (*13 Broad St, T: 01497 821556, www.tinto-house.co.uk; map p. 158, B2*). The **Seven Stars** has a swimming pool and sauna (*11 Broad St, T: 01497 820886; www.thesevenstars.co.uk; map p. 158, B2*). **Kilvert's Hotel** is a friendly, informal set-up with a large secluded garden (*Bullring, T: 01497 821042, www.kilverts.co.uk; map p. 159, C2*).

Among the B&Bs and self-catering options, **Oxford Cottage**, run by Ed Moore and Linda Webb, is outstanding (*Oxford Rd, T: 01497 820008, www.oxfordcottage.co.uk; map p. 159, D2*). The **Old Workhouse** in Union Mews offers a self-contained cottage (call Phil Sayce, *T: 07740 632950*).

A comprehensive 60-page booklet giving full accommodation listings is available free of charge from the Tourist Information Bureau on Oxford Rd (*T: 01497 820144, www.hay-on-wye.co.uk; map p. 158, B3*).

Many of the pubs and inns in the environs of Hay also offer rooms. One of the most charming places to stay, if you are in a small group, is the cottage at **Maesyronnen Chapel**, which is run by the Landmark Trust (*bookings. landmarktrust.org.uk*; sleeps 4). Other places with famous associations are the **Baskerville Hall Hotel** in Clyro (*T: 01497 820033, www.baskervillehall.co.uk; see p. 109*) and **The Grange** guest-house at Capel-y-ffin, run by the descendants of Eric Gill (*T: 01873 890215, www.grangetrekking.co.uk*). The latter is particularly suitable for horse-lovers. **Old Gwernyfed** near Felindre (*map p. 156, B2*) is also available for rent (sleeps 12; *www.oldgwernyfed.co.uk*).

LOCAL INFORMATION

Tourist Information Bureau
In the Craft Centre (Canol Crefft) on Oxford Rd (*open daily in summer 10–1 & 2–5; winter 11–1 & 2–4; T: 01497 820144, www.hay-on-wye.co.uk; map p. 158, B3*). There is internet access on two terminals costing (at the time of writing) 75p for 15mins. There is a helpful stock of free leaflets and booklets alongside useful books and maps for sale.

Banks
- Barclays Bank, Broad St;
- HSBC, High Town;
- NatWest Bank, Oxford Rd.

All three banks have cashpoints. During the Guardian Hay Festival, they are apt to run out of money.

Public Library

The library on Chancery Lane has a well-stocked local history section. The staff are friendly and helpful. There are computer terminals and it is sometimes possible to use these for internet access by arrangement (*T: 01497 820847*).

Guided Tours

Robert Soldat, historian and author of *A Walk Round Hay*, gives guided tours of Hay and its environs. He can be reached through the Tourist Information Bureau (*T: 01497 820144*).

PUBLIC TRANSPORT

By rail and bus

The nearest railway station to Hay is at Hereford, from where buses run by Stagecoach and Yeomans connect to Hay (*journey time 50mins*). During the Hay Festival, special buses link Hereford rail and bus stations with the Festival site and there is a shuttle from the centre of Hay (*see the Festival website for details; www.hayfestival.com*).

Bus no. 39 on weekays and 39A on Sundays and Bank Holidays serves Dorstone (*15mins*) and Peterchurch (*30mins*) in the Hereford direction, and Glasbury Bridge (*10mins*) and Felinfach (*30mins*) in the Brecon direction. From Glasbury Bridge it is 30–40mins' walk to Maesyronnen Chapel. The bus stop in Hay is by the Craft Centre on Oxford Rd.

Taxis

Glasbury Taxis can be reached on T: 0800 234 3337 or T: 07880 547337, and Taxius on T: 07760 456324.

OUTDOOR SPORTS

Walking and cycling

For maps, hiking boots, thick socks, waterproofs and the like, go to **Golesworthy** (est. 1877) at 17 Broad St or **P.S.M. Outdoors** at 7 Castle St. The best **hiking map** of the area is in the Ordnance Survey's Explorer series, Sheet OL13, Brecon Beacons National Park/Eastern Area. See www.walkingbritain.co.uk for suggested walks, distances and difficulty ratings.

    Drover Holidays offer bicycles for hire, and have a shop where you can buy bike kit at 3 Oxford Rd (*T: 01497 821134, info@droverholidays.co.uk, www.droverholidays.co.uk*).

Boat Hire

Jim and Pat Gamon operate **Paddles and Pedals**, hiring out canoes and kayaks by the day and half-day (*T: 01497 820604*). You can leave your car in the free riverside car-park and elect to be picked up by Jim or Pat after a strenuous trip downstream. The Wye Valley is rich in wildlife and it is possible to see herons, cormorants, swans, kingfishers and sometimes otters.

Fishing

There is excellent fishing along the banks of the Wye upstream from Hay Bridge to Warren Cottage. Permits are required and can be obtained from Golesworthy at 17 Broad St (*T: 01497 820491*).

FOOD FOR PICNICS

The **bakery** on Castle St sells fresh bread, cakes, tarts etc, as well as Welsh *bara brith*, boxes of chocolates, jams, marmalades and lemon curd. Opposite it is the small **Spar supermarket**—'good old Spar', as it is known locally—a useful shop for basics (it also stays open late).

For ready-made sandwiches, there is the **Sandwich Cellar** (*see p. 126*). **Xtreme OrganiX** at 10b Castle St is excellent if you're a foodie staying in self-catering accommodation. The deli and takeaway has won a clutch of awards and sells meat from its organic farm in Llanigon. There is a **grocer's shop** on Church St, and **Hay Whole Foods and Deli** at 41 Lion St has a good selection food and wine. Hay has two **butcher's shops** for freshly-cut ham, pork pies etc: Gibbons on Castle St and smallfarms on Broad St. The **Fudge Shop** at the Craft Centre sells what its name suggests, in all its manifold varieties.

FESTIVALS & EVENTS

For the Guardian Hay Festival, held every year in May–June, see p. 85. While this might be the most famous event held in Hay, it is by no means the only one. Indeed, Hay and its immediate area offer a plethora of festivals throughout the year. Events include:

Borderlines Film Festival:
The largest rural film festival in Britain, launched in 2003, Borderlines shows a cosmopolitan mix of new releases and classics. There is a good selection of associated events, sometimes featuring A-list headline speakers. The industry takes the festival seriously. It is an achievement for up-and-coming film-makers to have their work aired at Borderlines. The festival takes place in Feb–March at

Steam-powered roller at the Vintage Rally on Boatside Farm.

venues all over Shropshire, Herefordshire and the Mid Wales borders. For details see www.borderlinesfilmfestival.co.uk. The Hay venue is The Screen at Hay (*Parish Hall, Lion St, T: 01497 831189; map p. 159, C2*).

Hay-on-Wye Food Festival: Held in June in Memorial Square (*map p. 159, C2*). For information, contact the Tourist Information Bureau (*see p. 132 or T: 01874 624979*). This is a superb chance to sample home-made and home-reared produce, as well as Welsh specialities (*see box opposite*).

Brecon Jazz: Held in August at four venues in Brecon. (*T: 01874 611622, www.breconjazz. org*).

Vintage Rally: Held in August at Boatside Farm, just outside Hay, this is one of the finest assemblies of large steam traction engines in Britain, with vintage cars, commercial vehicles, tractors, and museum-quality motor and pedal cycles. Added attractions include fair organs, books, bars, automobilia and the opportunity to take a helicopter ride over the

Wye. Call to check dates (*T: 01874 711110; map p. 157, C1*).

Winter Weeked of Literature: Held in November. See Hay Festival Website for details of this and may other cultural events through the year.

Hay-on-Wye Thursday Market: The busy traditional market is held every Thursday from 8am to mid-afternoon in Memorial Square, in the Butter Market and around the Town Clock. Stalls sell fresh fruit and vegetables, cakes and pies, fresh fish and game, clothing, antiques and bric-à-brac (*T: 01497 820590*).

There are **concerts at St Mary's Church** throughout the year (*T: 01497 820448, www.wayonhigh.org.uk*).

A HANDFUL OF WELSH DELICACIES

'Welsh Rabbit is amusing and right. Welsh Rarebit is stupid and wrong.' So said H.W. Fowler in the 1926 edition of the *Dictionary of Modern English Usage*. He sought to emphasise that cheese was the poor man's rabbit in Wales and put paid to notions that Rarebit is anything other than a corruption of Rabbit. We give credence to the *Betty Crocker Cookbook* that gives the simple explanation that Welsh peasants were forbidden to catch rabbits caught on the estates of the gentry. Melted cheese proved a safe and nutritous alternative to poaching. The earliest mention of melted cheese in Britain is in Andrew Boorde's *Fyrst Boke of the Introduction of Knowledge* ➤

Leeks: the Welsh national vegetable and a key ingredient of Cawl.

(1542): 'I am a Welshman, I do love cause boby, good roasted cheese' (cause boby, in Welsh *caws pobi*, meaning 'baked cheese'). Of interest is a modern variant on the Welsh borders, where tomato soup is blended with cheese prior to roasting, creating the Blushing Bunny. A shy girl will invite the boy she has designs on to sample her Blushing Bunny. Depending on his response, she may also offer him her speckled fruit cake, Bara Brith (the secret of a good one is to soak the dried fruit in tea the night before)—if he is from South Wales he will doubtless retort that Bara Brith is a term used only in the north, and that if she wants to please him she must offer *Teisen Dorth*. The crowning glory of their married life, especially in the wastes of winter, will of course be Cawl, the nutritious lamb broth with leeks. This is often served with crusty bread and cheddar. The word Cawl (it rhymes with Howell) is first recorded the 14th century. There is an amusing story about the Welsh king Gruffydd ap Llywelyn, son of Llywelyn ap Seisyll. Gruffydd, unlike his dynamic father was a weak, ineffectual boy, given to daydreaming. One day, as he was loafing around near the castle kitchens, he overheard the cook complaining that one piece of mutton kept rising to the surface of the pot, however often it was pushed down. Gruffydd took this as an omen that he too should rise against the odds. He pulled himself together and by 1055 he was king of all Wales.

FURTHER READING

Local History

A History of the Hay – Geoffrey L. Fairs. The 1972 hardback edition, rather than the later paperback, remains a definitive guide to the history of Hay and its buildings. The documentary material is very fine. Much moving material is quoted, particularly in relation to poverty in Hay over the centuries.

A Walk Around Hay – Robert Soldat. A short and useful guide outlining two walks, inner and outer, to take in Hay-on-Wye.

My Kingdom of Books – Richard Booth. An entertaining and at times engagingly self-deprecating account of the King of Hay's career as book-dealer and monarch. Required reading for aspiring booksellers and those intending to transform their own town into a booktown along Hay lines.

Wisps of Hay, with other chaff – Cyril Marwood: An

eccentric and whimsical little volume containing vivid descriptions of Hay, its people and buildings. There is a memorable passage in which a telephone receiver is held at arm's length out of a window at Kilvert's in order to demonstrate to a disbelieving listener the intrusive strike of the Town Clock.

Nobody had heard of Hay: the Hay-on-Wye book that celebrates the Millennium – Karl Showler, Robert Soldat and others: The lively and informative introduction by Showler and Soldat covers the history of Hay from the complexities of the Welsh Marcher lords to the present day. This is a valuable book that pub- lishes some for the most part unedited transcripts of reminiscences by local people. These are by turns moving and funny.

Old Hay in Pictures and Prints – Eric Pugh. Album of old photographs of Hay. Available from Pembertons bookshop on High Town.

Planet Hay – Huw Parsons. Album of posed and candid shots of Hay and its characters (the author is a photographer and a local) accompanied by readable and engaging text.

The Curate's Kingdom – Jack and Rita Tait. 'A Year in the Life of St Mary's Parish Church, with Poodle Curate Jimmy', with a Comm- endation by the Archbishop of Canterbury. Photographs and text featuring the Vicar of Hay, Fr Richard Williams. Highlights include a snap of his poodle with Desmond Tutu.

Eric Gill and David Jones at Capel-y-Ffin – Jonathan Miles. A comprehensive look at Gill's sojourn in Wales.

Kilvertiana

Selections from the Diary of the Rev. Francis Kilvert, 1870–79 (Paperback) – Francis Kilvert, Ed. William Plomer, Pimlico 1999. This single-volume edition of the diaries (*see p. 111*) remains the best travelling companion. The three-volume indexed edition was repinted by O'Donoghue Books in 2006 and is stocked by many of the bookshops in Hay.

After Kilvert – A.L. Le Quesne. The Shrewsbury School history master's literary classic about the life and work of Kilvert, approached from a personal perspective with journals of the author's own sojourn in Ashbrook House. Le Quesne explains Kilvert's difficult status in the community and unravels some of the complexities of late Victorian provincial manners and prejudices.

At Home. Memoirs – William Plomer. The intriguing autobiography of the South African poet and editor who discovered and edited the Diaries of Francis Kilvert. The chapters 'The Typewritten Word' and 'The Curate of Clyro' are an illuminating account of the darkness of life as a pub-lisher's reader followed by the dawn of discovery. There are amusing recollections of Plomer's visits to Clyro, Hay and the surrounding area.

Folklore and legend

The Folklore and Witchcraft of Herefordshire – Ella Mary Leather. The great folklorist recounts local lore, including the fairies at Cusop Dingle and the Old Lady of the Black Mountain (*see p. 96*).

A Nest of Singing Birds: The Life and Work of Ella Mary Leather – Lavender Jones. An insight into Leather's research, including accounts of her field trips in Herefordshire with Ralph Vaughan Williams in search of folk songs and melodies.

The Mabinogion is published by Oxford World Classics in a translation by Sioned Davies. The eleven prose stories are the storehouse of Welsh literature, drawing on pre-Christian myth and medieval legend. A good companion for forays into the Black Mountains and the twilight landscape of old Radnorshire.

Fiction

On the Black Hill – Bruce Chatwin. A masterpiece set in a rural Wales closely resembling the environs of Hay. The novel tells the story of two twin brothers who work a farm. An unsettling saga of back-biting, frustration and resentment is played out against the backdrop of a tiny community in a remote location. The setting is stark and exposes the bare bones of love, jealousy, cruelty, spirituality and death.

Resistance – Owen Sheers. A novel set in the border country around Hay which imagines what might have happened if the D-Day Landings had failed. Sheers is also the author of *White Ravens*, a contemporary recasting of stories from the *Mabinogion* (*see above*).

Lady of Hay – Barbara Erskine. Historical novel based imaginatively on the life of Maud de St Valery (*see p. 19*). In *The Warrior's Princess*, Erskine tells her version of the story of St Eigon (*see pp. 97–98*).

GLOSSARY

Apse, recessed area at the far east end of a church, either curved or square

Bailey, wall or palisade around the keep (motte; *qv*) of a medieval castle

Barge boards, woodwork, often decorative, used as trimming along the pitch (sloping sides) of a roof-end

Brecknockshire, historic county of Wales in which Hay is situated. In 1974 it was amalgamated with Radnorshire to form the county of Powys

Burgage, town house and its strip of land, or a plot abutting a town or village boundary, rented out by the lord of the manor

Capital, the top or 'head' of a column

Churchwarden Gothic, disparaging term for the Gothic Revival style, used to suggest that the Gothic style has been misapplied or clumsily put to use

Colonnette, small column with a decorative, not load-bearing, function

Chancel, the area at the liturgical east end of a church, where the high altar is placed and where the clergy officiates. It is usually separated from the nave by an archway, sometimes with a screen

Chapel of ease, place of worship in a situation accessible by those who cannot easily attend the main or parish church

Classical, in ancient Greece, the great age of sculpture and temple-building of the 5th–4th centuries BC; in a modern context it refers to art harking back to this style

Codex (pl. codices) medieval manuscript book

Conch, the half-dome of an apse (*qv*) or other curved recess

Cruck-frame, roughly triangular-shaped building

framework formed of two curved, whalebone-shaped timbers meeting at the top

Curtain wall, a wall that stretches between bastions, piers, pillars or other load-bearing elements, like a curtain across a doorway

Doric, order of ancient Greek architecture. True Doric is characterised by fluted columns with no base and a plain capital. Tuscan Doric columns are unfluted and stand on a base

Entasis, a design technique used in ancient Greece to counteract the optical illusion of inner sagging created by the repeated parallel lines of a row of columns. This involved giving the columns a slightly convex curvature

Eucharistic, pertaining to the Eucharist, that is Holy Communion, the partaking of the bread and wine

Evangelists, the authors of the four gospels, Matthew, Mark, Luke and John

Flemish bond, bricklaying technique where the bricks in each course (row) are placed alternately short (header)-long (stretcher)-short-long

Gothic, medieval style of architecture originating in northern Europe, characterised by pointed arches, vaulted interiors and traceried (*qv*) windows

Hipped roof, roof with four sloping sides, meeting not in a single ridge at the top but in 'hips' up the sides

Hogget, a lamb in its second spring or summer (i.e. older than a year) but before its second year when it becomes mutton. Others define it as a sheep from about 9 to 18 months of age (until it cuts two teeth). Kim Cardell in *Practical Sheep Keeping* writes that 'unfinished lambs are kept as stores and sold during late winter and early spring as hoggets to fill the gap before new season lamb becomes available'

Hood mould, carved or

moulded decorative band around the top of a door or window aperture

Incunabulum (pl. incunabula) any book printed in the same century as the invention of movable type (i.e. between 1450 and 1500)

King-post truss, form of roof structure where a horizontal tie beam has a vertical beam, the king-post, rising from it to the apex of the roof

Lady Chapel, chapel devoted to the worship of the Virgin

Lancet, slender, blade-shaped Gothic window aperture with a pointed arched head

Lych gate, gateway at the entrance to a graveyard or cemetery

Mabinogion, book of medieval Welsh myths (*see p. 142*)

Machicolations, holes in the floor of a parapet through which stones, boiling oil etc could be dropped on attackers. Victorian bell-towers commonly sport

faux machicolations

Madrasah, an Islamic theological school

Menhir, a standing stone, from the Celtic *men* ('stone') *hir* ('long')

Motte, man-made mound on which a fortress or keep was built

Nave, the central aisle of a church. Some church designs have only a nave, without aisles at the sides

Norman, style of architecture of the 11th and 12th centuries in northern Europe, characterised by massive pillars and rounded arches and window apertures

Pantocrator, literally 'He who controls all'; a representation of Christ in majesty, traditionally featured in the dome of Byzantine churches and in the apse of basilicas

Perpendicular, late Gothic style characterised by marked horizontals as well as verticals, creating a panelled effect

Radnorshire, historic county

of Wales contiguous with and north of Brecknockshire (*qv*)

Silures, tribal people of ancient South Wales

Reredos, decorative, free-standing screen behind the high altar

Romanesque, a synonym for Norman (*qv*)

Rood, a Cross, typically that hanging from the chancel arch of a church, or surmounting the screen that separates nave from chancel

Rusticated, clad with masonry that is not flush at the joints but cut with grooves or narrow channels

Sash window, window where the panes are set in two wooden panels running the entire width of the aperture, suspended on ropes within the frame, and opened by raising one over the other

Segmental arch, arch with a shallow-curved top, a segment of a circle

Sheela-na-gig, ancient fertility symbol found in Britain and Ireland in the form of a woman exposing her genitalia. They are commonly found on church doorways. There is a fine one at Kilpeck, 7½ miles southeast of Peterchurch

Stations of the Cross, small paintings, panels, or carvings placed around the walls of a church or chapel depicting scenes from Christ's journey to Calvary

Tracery, system of carved and moulded ribs within a window aperture dividing it into patterned sections

Tympanum (pl. tympana), the area between the top of a flat-topped door or window and a curved arch above it; also the triangular space enclosed by the mouldings of a pediment

Vexillatio, detachment of a Roman legion formed as a temporary task force. Each bore a *vexillum*, a standard with the emblem and name of the parent legion. A vexillation fortress is the fort occupied by such a detachment

WELSH PLACE NAMES IN THIS GUIDE

ABERGAVENNY: Mouth (*aber*) of the River Gavenny. In Welsh the town is known as Y Fenni (pron: *uh-venni*)

ABERHONDDU: (pron: *abber-hon-ðee*): Brecon, meaning Mouth (*aber*) of the River Honddu

AFON GWY: (pron: *avvon gooi*): the River Wye. From *afon* (river) and *gwy*, cognate with the word for 'meandering'

CAPEL-Y-FFIN: (pron: *cappel-uh-feen*): Chapel on the Border

CLAS-AR-WY: (pron: *clas-ar-ooi*): Glasbury. Meaning Monks' house (*clas*) on the Wye

CLEIRWY: (pron: *cleïr-ooi*): Clyro. From *cleir/claer* (bright) and *Wy*, the Wye

DULAS: (pron: *dilas*): Black Brook

EWYAS, VALE OF: (pron: *e-ooyas*): Sheep Area

FELINDRE: (pron: *vellin-dre*): Mill Town

FELIN FACH: (pron: *vellin-vach*): Little Mill

HEOL Y DWR: (pron: *heol-uh-doowr*): Water Street

LLANIGON: Holy place (*llan*) of Eigon (local pron: *eye-gon*)

LLANTHONY: (pron: *llan-thonni*): Holy place (*llan*) on the River Honddu

MAESYRONNEN: (pron: *mice-uh-ronnen*): Field of Ash Trees

Y GELLI: (pron: *uh-gelli*): 'The Grove', Hay-on-Wye

Y MYNYDDOEDD DUON: (pron: *uh-munn-uh-ðoið dee-on*) The Black Mountains

dd: *like the 'th' in then;* **th**: *like the 'th' in thin;* **ch**: *like the 'ch' in loch;* **ll**: *like an aspirated 'th' + 'l'*

INDEX

All booksellers are in capitals; major sights are in bold capitals. Where many references are listed, the main or explanatory one is shown in bold. Numbers in italics are picture references.

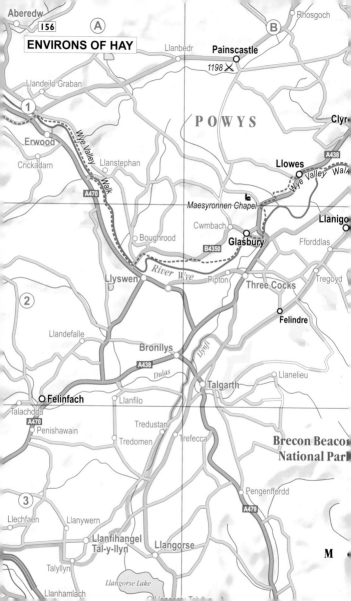

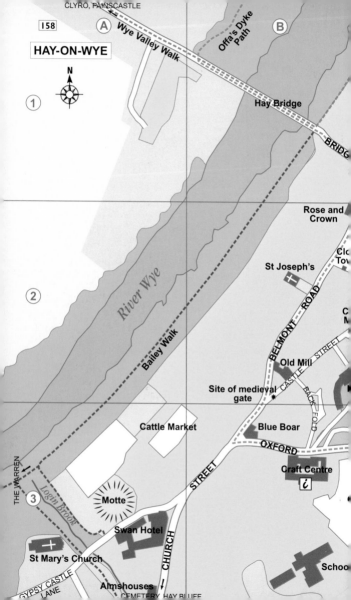

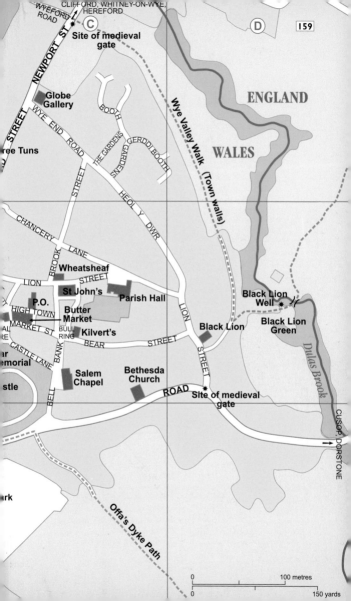

CLIFFORD, WHITNEY-ON-WYE,
HEREFORD

WYEFORD
ROAD

NEWPORT ST.

C

Site of medieval
gate

Globe
Gallery

BOOTH

ree Tuns

WYE END ROAD

THE GARDENS

GERDDI BOOTH

STREET

HEOL Y DWR

ENGLAND

WALES

Wye Valley Walk (Town walls)

D

CHANCERY LANE

BROOK

STREET

LION

Wheatsheaf

STREET

St John's

P.O.

HIGH TOWN

Butter
Market

BULL
RING

Kilvert's

MARKET ST.

BANK

BEAR

CASTLE LANE

emorial

stle

Parish Hall

LION STREET

Black Lion
Well

Black Lion

Black Lion
Green

STREET

Dulas Brook

Salem
Chapel

BELL

Bethesda
Church

ROAD

Site of medieval
gate

LION STREET

CUSOP, DORSTONE

rk

Offa's Dyke Path

0   100 metres

0   150 yards

contd. from p. 4

Editor: Annabel Barber

Maps by Dimap Bt, reproduced by permission of Ordnance Survey
on behalf of HMSO © Crown Copyright 2005. All rights reserved.
OS Licence No. 100043799;
Floor plan by Imre Bába
Architectural line drawings: Gabriella Juhász & Michael Mansell RIBA

Photo research, editing and pre-press: Hadley Kincade
Photographs by Jack and Rita Tait: pp. 6, 8–9, 36, 40, 98, 103, 106, 113,
122, 136; Tom Howells: pp. 28, 74; Annabel Barber: pp. 11, 14, 20, 45,
60, 68, 70, 75, 81, 91, 97, 138; © The Photolibrary Wales/Alamy/Red
Dot: p. 12; Stapleton Historical Collection / HIP / TopFoto: p. 25;
© Simon Whaley/Alamy/Red Dot: p. 38; © Dave G. Houser/Corbis/Red
Dot: p. 78; © Jeff Morgan 14/Alamy/Red Dot: pp. 87, 114;
Private Collection/ © The Fine Art Society, London, UK/The Bridgeman
Art Library: p. 105; Indianapolis Museum of Art, USA/Gift in memory of
Dr and Mrs Hugo Pantzer by their Children/The Brideman Art Library:
p. 108; © The De Morgan Centre, London/The Bridgeman Art Library:
p. 116; © Homer Sykes/Corbis/Red Dot: p. 119.

With thanks to Prudence Howells, Michael Partington,
Sian Roberts and John Vincent

Design: Anikó Kuzmich, Blue Guides; Pre-press: Anikó Kuzmich
Printed in Hungary by Dürer Nyomda Kft, Gyula

ISBN 978–1–905131–37–2

Your views on this book would be much appreciated. We welcome not
only specific comments, suggestions or corrections, but any more general
views you may have: how this book enhanced your visit, how it could have
been more helpful. Blue Guides authors and editorial and production team
work hard to bring you what we hope are the best-researched and best-
presented cultural, historical and academic guide books in the English
language. Please write to us by email (editorial@blueguides.com), via the
comments page on our website (www.blueguides.com) or at the address
given on p. 4. We will be happy to acknowledge useful contributions in the
next edition, and to offer a free copy of one of our titles.